Dining In-
Washington, D.C.
COOKBOOK

Vicky Bagley
and
Rona Cohen

Peanut Butter Publishing
Mercer Island, Washington

TITLES IN SERIES

Cover photograph by Kenneth Redding
Cover design and illustrations by Neil Sweeney

CONTENTS

PREFACE

Over the years we've watched Washington burgeon from a small, sleepy Southern town into an international center of politics and finance, culture and fine dining. There was a time when the good restaurants in D.C. could be counted on one hand. Now there is absolutely no way that one person can keep track of all the superb and different types of cuisine that are available. As our interests in the world and our travels throughout the world have increased, so have the restaurants in Washington.

Therefore, this is a sampling of much of the best—the top of the line, the elite. Each chef has his own style, each restaurant has its own special sparkle, its own certain message to impart on its guests. Many of the restaurants included in this collection can be tested against the best in the world and would come out with shining colors (and many "stars").

Be sure to take your time and peruse the recipes carefully. There are so many delights to behold, and so many wonderful recipes to try. As we worked with each of these talented people, we have had a personal cooking lesson. We have tried to transfer some of their vast experience and knowledge into the book for you to have and hold, too.

It would be somewhat unfair and more than a little redundant for us to begin recommending certain special recipes that are our favorites. Just rest assured that there are some easy ones and some that are quite difficult. There are several which will become old stand-bys in your kitchen, such as the *Chutney* from Shezan, and several that you may only make one time, with some effort and great delight, such as the *Terrine of Girolle Mushrooms with Lobster and Watercress Sauce* from Jean-Louis. And there are many, many that are, if not simple, at least not difficult.

Do enjoy these fruits of our adventures—and we did have some adventures in the preparation of this book. We know you will truly enjoy these recipes and the stories of the people behind them.

Rona Cohen

v

L'Auberge Chez François

Dinner for Six

La Salade de Poisson Marine

Les Crudités Obernoises

La Choucroute Alsacienne

Kugelhopf

Wine:

Riesling, Trimbach, Cuvée Frédéric Émile, 1977

François and Marie Antoinette Haeringer, Owners

François Haeringer, Executive Chef

Jacques Haeringer, Chef de Cuisine

L'AUBERGE CHEZ FRANÇOIS

Situated in Great Falls, Virginia, L'Auberge Chez François gives the impression of an Alsatian chalet. The hilly countryside surrounding the restaurant resembles northern France much more than its urban neighbor, Washington, D.C. Flowers adorn its entrance and, inside, a large open fireplace blazes all winter long. Year-round the tasteful decor, accented by floral tablecloths and green stemware, also contributes to the pristine mien of L'Auberge Chez François—rural elegance.

But it was not always so. At one time, Washington, D.C. was the home of the well-reputed restaurant named Chez François. Co-owner and Executive Chef François Haeringer, a native Frenchman, was very unhappy that the urban setting clashed with the quiet and graceful charm of his establishment. So he moved the entire operation some years ago to its present location. The decision to relocate reveals the essence of François's philosophy, that all parts must be considered equally important if the whole is to be a success. Thus the cuisine, the furnishings, the service, and the atmosphere are given no less attention than was the choice of locale. The menu at L'Auberge combines the old with the new, but François will not suggest to a patron that he might prefer one selection over another. He emphatically, and correctly, states instead that each and every selection is impeccably and equally a delight.

The restaurant is jointly owned by François and his wife Marie Antoinette Haeringer, and another family member, their son Jacques, holds the title of Chef de Cuisine. Jacques apprenticed in France and at other restaurants in Washington, D.C., as well as studying English at Virginia Commonwealth University, before he joined his parents' enterprise. He and his father work well and hard together in the kitchen, always striving to enhance and improve the established, excellent menu.

L'Auberge Chez François, because of the attention accorded each and every "part" of the restaurant, offers a perfect setting for an evening of tasteful and relaxed dining.

332 Springvale Road
Great Falls, Virginia

L'AUBERGE CHEZ FRANÇOIS

LA SALADE DE POISSON MARINE
Marinated Fish Salad

1 *pound fresh salmon*
1 *pound fresh sea scallops*
Juice of 10 lemons
Juice of 2 limes
2 *teaspoons salt*
½ *teaspoon pepper*
1 *teaspoon chopped fresh coriander (optional)*
1 *teaspoon chopped fresh dill*
1 *head Boston lettuce*

1 *head Belgian endive*
2 *tablespoons chopped shallots (optional)*
2 *tablespoons chopped parsley (optional)*
2 *tablespoons chopped green onions or chives (optional)*
Black caviar
2 *tablespoons vegetable oil*

1. Slice the salmon into slivers. Place the slivers and the scallops in separate deep earthenware bowls. Sprinkle evenly with lemon and lime juices and season with the salt, pepper, coriander, and dill. Cover and marinate overnight in the refrigerator.

2. Wash the Boston lettuce and the Belgian endive and dry completely. Place a bed of Boston lettuce on each of six chilled salad plates. Spread four spears of the Belgian endive over the lettuce leaves to form an "x." Layer the salmon over the endive, then the scallops over the salmon. If desired, garnish with a combination of the shallots, parsley, green onion or chives, and top each with about 1 teaspoon of the caviar. Pour about 1 teaspoon of the oil over each plate to moisten and glaze, and serve at once.

My father and I developed this recipe, among many others, using the wonderful seafood available here in the Chesapeake Bay area. I suggest you slice the scallops before marinating, if they are large.

LES CRUDITÉS OBERNOISES
Gruyère, Beets, Carrots, and Celery Root with Rémoulade Sauce

2 teaspoons finely minced onion
1 tablespoon peanut oil
1 teaspoon white wine vinegar
½ teaspoon salt
Freshly ground white pepper

1 pound Gruyère cheese
6 large fresh beets
6 large carrots
Salt to taste
4 medium-size celery roots
RÉMOULADE SAUCE
Fresh chopped parsley

1. Combine the onion, oil, vinegar, salt, and white pepper to form a dressing. Set aside.
2. Remove the rind from the Gruyère cheese and cut into julienne strips the size of matchsticks. Place in a bowl and gently toss with half the dressing.
3. Cook the beets in lightly salted boiling water about 35 to 45 minutes, or until done. Drain. When cool enough to handle, peel and slice into julienne strips. Place in a bowl and toss with the remaining dressing.
4. Peel the carrots and grate on a medium-size grater. Place in a bowl and season lightly with salt.
5. Peel the celery roots, cut into julienne strips, and place in a bowl. Add the Rémoulade Sauce and mix gently until well coated.
6. Arrange the Gruyère, beets, carrots, and celery root on a large platter in separate, carefully formed piles. Garnish generously with the chopped parsley and serve.

Celery root is also known as celeriac.

We often serve this to guests accompanied with a platter of our homemade pâtés. With warm French bread and wine, it becomes a meal in itself!

L'AUBERGE CHEZ FRANÇOIS

RÉMOULADE SAUCE

1 *cup mayonnaise*	*⅛ teaspoon sugar*
1½ *teaspoons dry mustard*	*½ teaspoon lemon juice*

Combine all ingredients in a deep bowl.

LA CHOUCROUTE ALSACIENNE
Alsatian Sauerkraut

5 *pounds sauerkraut*	1 *(2-pound) slab lean smoked bacon*
2 *tablespoons lard or butter*	2 *pounds smoked pork shoulder*
2 *medium-size onions, diced*	12 *small potatoes*
½ *teaspoon salt*	6 *frankfurters*
1½ *cups dry white wine (preferably Alsatian Riesling)*	2 *pounds Polish kielbasa sausage*
1 *cup Chicken Stock (see index)*	1 *teaspoon peanut oil*
Bouquet garni:	6 *bratwurst*
3 *cloves*	*Horseradish*
1 *bay leaf*	*Dijon mustard*
3 *cloves crushed garlic*	
½ *teaspoon thyme*	
12 *crushed juniper berries*	
10 *cracked peppercorns*	

1. Preheat oven to 350°.
2. Place the sauerkraut in a deep colander, drain well, and rinse several times. Squeeze until all moisture is removed. Blot dry with paper towels. Set aside.
3. Melt the lard in a deep, heavy saucepan and cook the diced onions until limp; do not brown. Add the sauerkraut, salt, wine, and chicken stock. Bring to a full boil. Bury the bouquet garni in the broth along with the bacon slab and the pork shoulder.
4. Cover the saucepan, place in preheated oven, and cook 1½ hours. Do not overcook; the sauerkraut should still be crisp.
5. While sauerkraut is cooking, boil the potatoes in a pot of salted water about 20 to 30 minutes, or until tender. Peel and keep warm.
6. About 10 minutes before the sauerkraut is ready, add the frankfurters and the Polish kielbasa, burying these in the hot sauerkraut so they absorb juice while they cook.
7. In an 8-inch sauté pan, heat the peanut oil and gently brown the bratwurst. Set aside.

8. Remove the pork and bacon from the saucepan and cut into thick slices. Place the sauerkraut on a large oval or rectangular platter. Arrange the pork and bacon slices with the sausages and boiled potatoes on top. Serve at once with the horseradish and Dijon mustard.

Note: To make the bouquet garni, place the herbs and spices in a 4-inch square of cheesecloth and tie with kitchen twine.

I was raised in Alsace, where this dish is customary. The juniper berries, which grow wild in forests and mountain ravines, add a distinctive flavor and, therefore, are essential. As it was in my native Alsace, this dish is ideal for the fall and winter.

KUGELHOPF

⅓ cup golden raisins
2 tablespoons kirsch
½ teaspoon unflavored gelatin
12 egg whites
2 tablespoons grated orange rind

2 teaspoons grated lemon rind
1 teaspoon vanilla extract
1¼ cups sugar
CARAMEL GLAZE
3 kiwi fruit, sliced

1. Place the raisins in a small cup and cover with the kirsch. Marinate overnight.

2. The next day, place the gelatin and 2 tablespoons water in a small saucepan. Stir to mix; let stand for 5 minutes, then place over very low heat. Stir constantly until the gelatin dissolves and the mixture becomes clear.

3. Preheat oven to 300°. Butter an 8-cup kugelhopf mold or 10-inch bundt pan and sprinkle with sugar.

4. In a large mixing bowl, combine the dissolved gelatin with the egg whites, fruit rinds, vanilla extract, and ½ teaspoon of the kirsch from the raisins. With an electric beater, beat at high speed until foamy. Add the sugar, a few tablespoons at a time, and continue to beat until the meringue forms stiff glossy peaks.

5. Drain the kirsch from the raisins and fold the raisins into the meringue. Spoon into the kugelhopf mold or bundt pan. Cut through the meringue with a rubber spatula to break up large air bubbles, then smooth the surface.

6. Place the filled mold into a larger baking pan at least 4 inches deep. Place together in the preheated oven. Pour water into the larger pan to a depth of 3 inches. Bake in preheated oven for 30 minutes, cover with foil to prevent rapid browning, and bake 30 minutes longer, or until a cake tester inserted into the center comes out clean.

7. Remove the mold or pan from the water and set on a wire rack. Immediately loosen the kugelhopf by running a knife around the edge and tube. This will prevent the kugelhopf from tearing as it cools and shrinks. Cool completely in the pan.

8. Pour the Caramel Glaze over the top and sides of the kugelhopf to cover entirely. Refrigerate 2 hours. If desired, garnish with the kiwi fruit before serving.

To serve the Kugelhopf, bring a sharp knife down on the glaze with a quick chopping stroke and slice.

A kugelhopf mold, referred to sometimes as a Turk's head pan, has a swirled, fluted dome shape. The kugelhopf itself is the hallmark of Alsatian bakers.

CARAMEL GLAZE

½ *cup sugar*   ½ *cup water*

Combine the sugar with the water in a small saucepan and cook over medium heat, occasionally shaking the pan, until the sugar melts and turns a golden brown. Remove from heat and pour over the Kugelhopf immediately.

Le Bagatelle

Dinner for Six

Salade de Coquilles Saint Jacques au Vinaigre d'Aneth

Suprême de Caneton aux Baies de Cassis et Navets Confits

Melée d'Endives, Haricots Verts, et Foie Gras à l'Huile de Noix

Gratin de Framboise aux Noisettes

Wines:

With the Scallops—Pouilly-Fuissé, Les Paulettes, 1979

With the Duckling—Château Gruaud-Larose, St.-Julien, 1971

With the Gratin—Domaine Chandon Brut

Robert Greault, Jacques Scarella, and Paul Zucconi, Owners
Robert Greault, Executive Chef
Michel Haudebert, Head Chef

LE BAGATELLE

Robert Greault opened his restaurant in 1972, envisioning for its decor the resplendent garden of the Jardin de Bagatelle in the Bois de Boulogne. He recreated the essential beauty of the garden for his restaurant and adopted the name of the garden. For his logo, he chose a single, long-stemmed rose against a field of white. The effect recalls an earlier Parisian elegance, appropriate to Robert's fine classical French cuisine and original creations.

For bon vivants, Le Bagatelle titillates the senses as it heightens an appreciation for the aesthetic. While sipping vintage wine, guests may notice why the atmosphere is bright and cheerful: sunshine filters through sheer, pale green drapes and illuminates the well appointed tables of white damask with contrasting chartreuse napkins. The chairs are upholstered in green and orange, and each table features the characteristic rose. All the tables are arranged in full view of a gazebo surrounded by white trellises with luxuriant plants weaving through the latticework. Within this uplifting floral freshness, Robert displays his culinary arts.

"I express myself with food," says Robert with animation and pride. Years of training and sojourns in famous restaurants worldwide have nurtured his talent and developed his sophistication. Not in the vanguard of nouvelle cuisine, Robert points out that "many professional chefs used long ago what is called nouvelle cuisine today." Robert respects the classical cuisine and never borrows traditional titles for his own creations.

Robert began his training in Paris where from 1950 to 1957, he was Chef de Partie at the Drouant, followed by a year at Maxim's. He spent the next year at L'Escargot, the legendary restaurant built during the reign of Henry II and now located in the heart of Les Halles, Paris's central open-air market. During the next phase of his career, he sojourned as Chef de Cuisine in Caracas, Venezuela, and in Papeete, Tahiti.

In 1969, he arrived in Washington from New York, by then an experienced executive chef, to resume that position in the Jockey Club. Three years later he established Le Bagatelle and presently is joining forces with his partners Jacques Scarella and Paul Zucconi to open La Colline near the Capitol in southeast Washington.

Le Bagatelle is putatively a bastion of the finest in French cuisine and M. Greault, a chef par excellence. Some say there is an intensity about this gracious gentleman that is breathtaking, and, though mellowed somewhat over the years, still a delight to behold.

2000 K Street, N. W.

SALADE DE COQUILLES SAINT JACQUES
AU VINAIGRE D'ANETH
Cold Long Island Bay Scallops with Dill Vinegar

1 green pepper	Salt and pepper
1 carrot	1½ pounds fresh bay scallops
1 red pimiento	DILL VINEGAR DRESSING
1 leek	(see next page)
½ cup water	Chilled lettuce leaves
1 cup dry white wine	
Bouquet garni:	
6 sprigs parsley	
1 bay leaf	
1 sprig thyme	

1. Finely julienne the vegetables. Bring the water and wine to a full boil with the bouquet garni. Plunge the vegetables into the boiling liquid and cook until the liquid returns to a boil. Remove the vegetables with a skimmer and plunge into cold water to arrest cooking. Season with the salt and pepper and cool in a deep bowl.

2. Return broth to a boil and add the scallops. Cook for 30 seconds, then drain and cool in a separate bowl.

3. Pour equal parts of the Dill Vinegar Dressing over the vegetables and the scallops. Cover each bowl and marinate in refrigerator for a minimum of 1 hour.

4. Cover six salad plates with the lettuce leaves. Divide the vegetables over. Top with the scallops. Serve immediately.

It is extremely important that the vegetables be of the same width and that you barely cook them. The scallops should be tiny and also barely cooked. This is a wonderful dish for a picnic, by the way.

DILL VINEGAR DRESSING

⅓ cup dill vinegar
½ teaspoon salt
⅛ teaspoon pepper

1 cup peanut oil
1 tablespoon chopped fresh dill

1. In a small bowl, whisk together the vinegar, salt, and pepper. Beating vigorously, slowly add the oil to the vinegar.
2. Add the dill and taste for seasoning.

SUPRÊME DE CANETON AUX BAIES DE CASSIS ET NAVETS CONFITS
Breast of Duckling with Black Currants and Baby Turnips

3 (4½ to 5-pound) ducklings
1 quart black currants, canned
3 medium-size turnips, peeled

½ pound unsalted butter
Salt and pepper
1½ cups DUCK STOCK
1 tablespoon cassis or blackberry liqueur

1. Remove the breasts whole from the ducklings, leaving breastbones intact. Do not skin. Place the breasts in a deep pan. Drain the currants, reserving the juice, and set aside. Pour the juice over the breasts. Cover and marinate 2 hours in the refrigerator. Turn occasionally so breasts marinate evenly.
2. Cut the turnips into 36 balls, using a melon baller. Melt 4 tablespoons of the butter in a small saucepan over low heat. Sauté balls until tender; do not overcook. Remove and keep covered.
3. Preheat oven to 325°.
4. Remove breasts from juice and drain. Reserve juice. Cut each breast in half down the center through the breastbone. Melt ½ cup of the butter in a 10-inch ovenproof sauté pan. Brown the breast halves skin-side down. Place pan in preheated oven and bake until breasts are tender, about 25 minutes. Remove.

5. Remove breasts from pan. Season lightly with the salt and pepper and keep warm.

6. Deglaze the sauté pan with the berry juice and Duck Stock. Reduce slowly until sauce begins to thicken. Do not boil. Add the cassis and 2 tablespoons of the butter. Add the currants and a dash more salt and pepper.

7. Remove skin and bones from breasts. Thinly slice each half and arrange on six warmed dinner plates. Pour the cassis sauce over each plate and serve. The turnip balls should be placed alongside the duckling but not napped with the sauce.

DUCK STOCK

6 to 7 pounds duck bones, scraps, and giblets (except liver)	2 cups white wine
1 tablespoon oil	2 sprigs parsley
1 large onion, sliced	2 bay leaves
2 carrots, chopped	1/8 teaspoon thyme
2 leeks, washed and sliced	1 tablespoon salt
3 stalks celery, chopped	1 teaspoon white pepper

1. Trim fat and remove skin from the duck bones and scraps. Wash well. Set aside with giblets.

2. Pour the oil into a 6 to 8-quart stockpot, then add the onion, carrots, leeks, and celery. Cook over moderate heat about 3 minutes. Place the duck bones, scraps, and giblets on top of the vegetables. Sweat together over moderate heat about 10 minutes. Shake the pan occasionally; do not stir.

3. Add the wine, 3 cups warm water, and seasonings and bring to a full boil. Remove any scum that surfaces. Lower heat, cover, and simmer about 3 hours.

4. Remove from heat and allow to cool. Strain through a fine sieve into a clean pot. Reheat stock or freeze for future use.

LE BAGATELLE

MELÉE D'ENDIVES, HARICOTS VERTS, ET FOIE GRAS A L'HUILE DE NOIX

2 *heads Belgian endive*
½ *pound extra-fine fresh*
   string beans
3 *ounces pâté de foie gras*

12 *walnut halves*
WALNUT OIL DRESSING
Salt and pepper

1. Cut the bases off the endives and wash carefully, separating the leaves. Dry and keep chilled.
2. Remove the stems and ends from the green beans and wash well. In a small saucepan, bring 1 cup of salted water to a full boil. Submerge the beans and boil 4 to 5 minutes until crisp-tender. Pour beans into a colander and douse with cold water to arrest cooking. Drain well.
3. Slice the pâté de foie gras into thin strips and set aside. In a large bowl, combine the endive, beans, and pâté carefully with the Walnut Oil Dressing.
4. Divide the salad among six chilled salad plates and sprinkle with the walnut halves. Serve at once.

WALNUT OIL DRESSING

Juice of 1 lemon
¼ *teaspoon salt*

Pinch of white pepper
¼ *cup walnut oil*

1. Whisk together the lemon juice, salt, and pepper in a small bowl.
2. Add the oil slowly while whisking vigorously.
3. Taste for seasoning and correct, if necessary.

GRATIN DE FRAMBOISE AUX NOISETTES
Gratin of Fresh Raspberries with Hazelnuts

1 *quart fresh raspberries*	1 *cup whipping cream*
3 *egg yolks*	6 *tablespoons raspberry*
½ *cup sugar*	*liqueur*
¼ *cup all-purpose flour,*	*Butter, softened*
sifted	½ *cup coarsely chopped*
1 *pint milk*	*hazelnuts*
½ *vanilla bean, or ½ teaspoon*	*Sifted confectioners' sugar*
vanilla extract	

1. Wash the raspberries, discarding any that are bruised. Drain and keep chilled.

2. In a small bowl, beat the egg yolks and sugar until they are white. Add the flour to the eggs, but do not overmix.

3. In a small saucepan, bring the milk and vanilla to a boil. Pour slowly over yolk mixture so yolks do not cook. Return custard mixture to saucepan and bring to a boil, mixing well. Boil 1 minute. Remove from heat and cool completely. Discard the vanilla bean, if used.

4. Preheat oven to 350°. In a chilled bowl, beat the cream until stiff. Blend the cooled custard with the raspberry liqueur. Fold in the whipped cream and the raspberries, being careful not to break the whole berries.

5. Pour into a buttered 12-inch or 14-inch au gratin dish and sprinkle with the hazelnuts. Bake in preheated oven 7 minutes. Remove.

6. Dust with the confectioners' sugar and serve warm.

If you use a vanilla bean, split it down the side so that its essence permeates the milk.

el Bodegón

Dinner for Four

Sangría

Huevos a la Flamenca

Gazpacho Andaluz

Ensalada Mallorquina

Paella Valenciana

Flan

Beverages:

Before dinner—Tío Pepe Dry Sherry

After dinner—Cuarenta y Trés (43) liqueur

Ebé Martínez-Vidal, Malisa Tripoda, and José Lopez-Guerra, Owners

Ebé Martínez-Vidal, Executive Chef

Justino Alves, Chef

EL BODEGÓN

El Bodegón aptly borrowed its name from the Spanish word "bodega," or "wine cellar," a place where one goes to relax over a glass of wine. The ambiance of the restaurant, characterized by cozy surroundings and background flamenco music, is so authentic that one could easily imagine himself in some Spanish township instead of an American megalopolis. Then, the warm and attentive service provided compels one to relax and enjoy. El Bodegón is more than a wine cellar, however, because it offers exquisite Spanish cuisine as well as drink, both of which are prepared with impeccable imagination and care.

Ownership of the twenty-year old Washington landmark was assumed two years ago by Ebé Martínez-Vidal, Malisa Tripoda, and Ebé's son José Lopez-Guerra. They have maintained the traditions which made the original restaurant so popular while simultaneously infusing their own gifted spirit into the restaurant's character. Regular patrons, for example, can choose for their dining pleasure either the traditional fare or newly introduced concoctions invented by Executive Chef Ebé or Chef Justino Alves, such as Ebé's Chocolate Mousse Cake or Lomo de Cerdo a la Reina (pork loin served with a rich sauce and vegetables). A popular lunchtime course is the complimentary "Tapas," an appetizer of varied marinated vegetables or meats. One of these, Papas a la Brava, which consists of cooked potato slices in a hot brava sauce, is guaranteed to ignite any palate.

The owners wish their guests to feel relaxed, and happy, and at home at El Bodegón. Their technique for serving "porron," a house specialty, exemplifies how carefully the staff attends to the guests' needs. After bringing the wine to the table, the waiter, or sometimes even José, skillfully and gracefully positions the carafe above the patron's head. He then tips it so that the wine flows in a long arc through the air to its destination—the guest's mouth. So engaging and so intimate is this bit of theatrics that it insures that all around, if they haven't already, sit back, relax, and enjoy. And that is exactly what one *should* do at a "wine cellar."

1637 R Street, N.W.

SANGRÍA

1½ ounces Spanish brandy	3 thin slices fresh lemon
1½ ounces triple sec	1 cup club soda
3 thin slices fresh orange	Ice cubes
3 thin slices fresh apple	¾ bottle red Rioja wine

1. Pour the brandy and triple sec into a 1-quart pitcher. Add the sliced fruit, club soda, and ice cubes.
2. Fill with the Rioja wine and stir well. Serve.

Sangría is a delightful drink to serve any time of day, any time of year. Add fruits of the season if you wish, but keep the rest of the ingredients the same.

HUEVOS A LA FLAMENCA
Eggs Baked in Sauce

2 tablespoons butter	2 tablespoons sherry
2 tablespoons olive oil	½ tablespoon tomato sauce
1 small onion, finely chopped	¾ teaspoon salt
1 medium-size green pepper, seeded and cubed	Freshly ground black pepper
¼ cup cubed Serrano ham	4 eggs
1 medium tomato, peeled, seeded, and chopped	1 tablespoon finely chopped parsley
2 tablespoons cooked peas	1 red pepper or pimiento, cut in 8 long slices
¼ cup cooked asparagus tips	
4 thin slices plus 4 thick slices chorizo sausage	

1. Preheat oven to 375°. Butter four individual baking dishes or ramekins 4 inches by 1½ inches with 1 tablespoon of the butter. Melt the remaining 1 tablespoon in a small saucepan.

(continued next page)

2. Heat the olive oil in a heavy 4-quart saucepan and add the onion, green pepper, and ham. Simmer 3 minutes. Add the tomato and stir 3 minutes. Add the peas, asparagus tips, the thin slices of chorizo, sherry, tomato sauce, ¼ teaspoon salt, and pepper. Bring to a simmer and cook 5 minutes longer.

3. Divide the mixture between the four baking dishes. Break 1 raw egg into each dish, centering it in the sauce. Baste with the melted butter and season with the remaining ½ teaspoon salt, pepper, and parsley.

4. Bake in preheated oven 6 minutes or until the whites of the eggs are set. Remove.

5. Garnish each dish with a thick slice of the chorizo and slices of red pepper. Serve immediately.

This is the most popular appetizer served in Madrid, requested everywhere. It has a great following in Spain and here at El Bodegón as well. It is excellent for lunch and, of course, for the ever-popular American brunch. Serve with sangría and flan for a fabulous combination.

GAZPACHO ANDALUZ
Cold Tomato Soup

2 large firm red tomatoes, cut into wedges
1 medium-size green pepper
1 medium-size cucumber
1½ tablespoons tomato paste
½ cup finely chopped bread crumbs
¼ teaspoon cumin
1 clove garlic, crushed

1½ tablespoons mayonnaise
1½ tablespoons red wine vinegar
2½ cups canned chicken broth
½ teaspoon salt
Freshly ground black pepper
1 small onion, chopped
1 cup TOASTED CROUTONS

1. Purée the tomato wedges in an electric blender. Remove the seeds of the green pepper and dice the rind. Thickly slice half of the cucumber. Add the diced green pepper and cucumber to the blender and purée. Add the tomato paste and bread crumbs and purée. Pour into a large bowl.

2. In a small bowl, combine the cumin, garlic, mayonnaise, and vinegar. Combine chicken broth and seasoned mayonnaise with the puréed tomato mixture. Season with the salt and pepper. Cover and refrigerate at least 2 or 3 hours.

3. Just before serving, stir the soup well and pour into four chilled soup bowls. Finely chop the remaining green pepper and chop the remaining cucumber. Combine the green pepper, cucumber, onion, and Toasted Croutons. Sprinkle over the cold soup and serve at once.

Gazpacho is one of the most refreshing soups found anywhere. This recipe is typical of Andalucía in the south of Spain. It must be served ice cold! If you cannot find good fresh tomatoes, try some of the excellent canned Spanish tomatoes on the market. They are far superior to the hot-house variety.

TOASTED CROUTONS

6 slices bread (preferably   2 tablespoons olive oil
  French or Italian)

1. Trim crusts from the bread and discard. Dice the bread into ¼-inch cubes.

2. Place a 10-inch sauté pan over moderate heat. Add the oil and heat well but not to smoking point. Add the cubes to the pan and shake over heat, stirring constantly with a large wooden spoon. Lift the cubes from the bottom so that all will become coated with the oil.

3. Continue stirring until bread cubes become crisp and golden. Remove and lay on paper towels to drain excess oil.

Fresh bread is sometimes difficult to slice. The best croutons are made with bread that is not extremely fresh, preferably day-old.

ENSALADA MALLORQUINA

1½ teaspoons salt
20 medium-size fresh shrimp,
    peeled and deveined
2 red apples
    Juice of ½ lemon
1 ripe avocado
1 cup diced fresh pinepple
¼ cup HOMEMADE
    MAYONNAISE

¼ cup whipping cream
    Freshly ground black pepper
1 large head Bibb lettuce,
    washed and dried
½ cup coarsely chopped
    walnuts

1. In a medium saucepan, bring cold water to a rolling boil with 1 teaspoon of the salt. Add the shrimp and cook about 6 minutes until just pink. Do not overcook. Remove. Drain well and pat dry with paper towels.
2. Core and dice the apples, leaving the skin intact. Toss with the lemon juice in a large mixing bowl. Peel and dice the avocado. Add to the apples with the pineapple. Add the drained shrimp, blend together, and cover.
3. In a small jar with a secure lid, combine the Homemade Mayonnaise, whipping cream, ½ teaspoon of the salt, and pepper. Tighten the lid and shake vigorously to blend. Pour over salad and toss.
4. Pile the salad in the center of four salad plates layered with the lettuce leaves. Top with the walnuts and serve immediately.

This is one of my original recipes. It is excellent for a luncheon, especially when you remember to serve a pitcher of sangría with it. Never be afraid to mix unusual ingredients; you never know what you might create!

HOMEMADE MAYONNAISE

2 *egg yolks*
½ *teaspoon salt*
½ *teaspoon dry mustard*

⅛ *teaspoon white pepper*
2 *teaspoons vinegar*
1 *cup olive oil*

1. With a rotary beater, beat the egg yolks well in a large mixing bowl. Add the salt, mustard, pepper, and 1 teaspoon of the vinegar. Beat together.
2. Gradually add the oil, one drop at a time, while beating, until about half the oil has been incorporated. Add ½ teaspoon of the vinegar, then continue with the oil.
3. When all the oil has been incorporated, add the remaining ½ teaspoon vinegar and blend. The mayonnaise should be thick and creamy.

PAELLA VALENCIANA
Chicken and Seafood Combination

4 *clams*
12 *mussels*
    Canned chicken broth,
    if needed
2 *tablespoons olive oil*
8 *small pieces fresh chicken*
1 *teaspoon salt*
½ *cup ham, cut into thin*
    strips
1 *medium-size green pepper,*
    seeded and chopped
1 *onion, chopped*
3 *medium-size squid, cleaned*
    and sliced into rings
1 *clove garlic, crushed*
2 *large tomatoes, peeled,*
    seeded, and chopped

1 *teaspoon paprika*
4 *small, firm fish fillets*
    (preferably haddock)
    Large pinch of saffron,
    soaked in 2 tablespoons
    warm water
2 *cups converted rice*
    Freshly ground black pepper
8 *medium-size shrimp,*
    shelled and deveined
3 *tablespoons cooked peas*
2 *canned pimientos, thinly*
    sliced
2 *tablespoons finely*
    chopped parsley
1 *lemon, cut in thin wedges*

(continued next page)

1. Scrub the clams and mussels thoroughly. Discard any that are opened. Fill a deep pot with water to 1 inch in depth and bring to a full boil. Add the clams and mussels. Cover and steam 7 to 8 minutes, or until shells have opened. Remove from broth and set aside.

2. Strain the cooking liquid into a 2-cup measure. If there is not enough liquid to measure 2 cups, add the chicken broth to make up the difference. Set aside.

3. Add the olive oil to a paella pan heated over medium flame and heat well. Sauté the chicken in the hot oil about 5 minutes, turning as the pieces brown. Season with the salt. Add the sliced ham and sauté 5 minutes longer. Cover and cook about 15 minutes, or until the chicken is tender.

4. Add the green pepper, onion, squid, and garlic, tossing well to coat thoroughly with the oil. Stir in the tomatoes, paprika, fish fillets, saffron with liquid, rice, and several grinds of the pepper.

5. Raise heat and add the 2 cups broth and 2 cups boiling water. Bring quickly to a boil, stirring once. Reduce heat and let liquid simmer gently for 10 minutes. Do not cover pan or stir the rice again.

6. Add the shrimp, pushing them down into the other ingredients. Simmer 5 minutes. Add the reserved clams and mussels in their shells and the peas. Cook 10 minutes longer, or until the rice has absorbed all the liquid and is fluffy. If undercooked, the grains of rice will tend to stick together. Remove from heat, cover, and allow to rest 5 minutes.

7. Heat the pimientos in their own juice and then drain. Sprinkle the paella with the parsley and garnish the top with the pimiento and lemon. Serve directly from the pan.

It is with great pride that I share with you this recipe, the pride of El Bodegón. This is the famous paella of Valencia, the most colorful and, I believe, the tastiest paella of all the many paellas in Spain. It is a masterpiece of color and flavor.

EL BODEGÓN

FLAN

1 cup sugar
2 cups milk
½ vanilla bean
3 eggs
Pinch of salt

½ cup whipping cream
1 tablespoon sifted
  confectioners' sugar
1 drop vanilla extract

1. Preheat oven to 350°.
2. Melt ½ cup of the sugar in a heavy skillet over low heat, stirring constantly, until the sugar melts and turns a light caramel color. Immediately pour a spoonful of the hot syrup into the bottom of each of four custard cups, stirring gently. Cool slightly.
3. In a large saucepan, bring the milk to simmering point, then add the remaining sugar. Simmer 5 minutes. Remove milk from heat and add the vanilla bean. Cool about 8 to 10 minutes.
4. In a deep bowl, beat the eggs lightly with the salt. Slowly add the milk, stirring constantly. Using a fine sieve, strain the custard mixture into the prepared cups. Place the cups in a rectangular baking pan and fill the pan almost to the top with tepid water.
5. Place pan in preheated oven and bake 35 to 40 minutes, or until custard tests done when a table knife is inserted diagonally and comes out clean. Immediately remove pan from oven and cups of custard from water. Refrigerate 3 hours before serving.
6. Beat the cream with the confectioners' sugar until stiff and mix in the vanilla extract. When ready to serve, invert custard cups on four serving plates and shake very gently. Remove cups and garnish the flan with the slightly sweetened whipped cream, if desired.

This is the old-fashioned way to make flan, a traditional favorite from Spain and an original recipe from my grandmother. It is elegant and simple and a delightful finish to a spicy, or even not-so-spicy, Spanish dinner. For color, I sometimes garnish the plates with a carefully cleaned fresh flower nestled in one side of the whipped cream.

Cantina d'Italia

Dinner for Six

Risotto Barolo

Zuppa Minestra di Pomodori

Insalata di Càvolo Rosso con Bagna Cauda

Costolétte alla Valdostana

Spinaci alla Piemontèis

Soma d'Ai

Crostini all'Aglio e Mozzarella

Zabaglione

Beverages:
Before dinner—Grappa d'Alba
With dinner—Gattinara

Joseph Muran de Assereto, Owner and Executive Chef

CANTINA D'ITALIA

C antina d'Italia, the first Northern Italian restaurant established in Washington, D.C., features authentic cuisine from Piemonte, Val d'Aosta, Liguria and other regions in the northern peninsula. At the Cantina, ethnicity is the keynote. Guests dine in a cultural enclave where the menus retain spellings in the dialect and where the flavor of the provinces comes through the Mediterranean decor—the fountainheads, tapestries, and other memorabilia adorning stucco walls.

With imaginations and appetites whetted by this old world ambiance, guests anticipate a mouth-watering repast. Patrons of longer standing know that the freshest meats and produce arrive every morning and that all dishes are prepared to order. And, the staff are quick to point out, the chef uses no commercially prepared ingredients.

Indeed, principal credit for the Cantina's reputation as Washington's hallmark of Northern Italian cuisine goes to chef Joseph d'Assereto. A Francophile of Italian descent, Joseph discovered an inborn talent for cooking while working at Brennan's in New Orleans shortly after the Second World War. Years later, he accepted a position at the Cantina and, not long after, took over the kitchen. He brought to it a persistent creativity, especially a canniness about seeing beyond the accepted to try new combinations. Through his diligent research to preserve the authenticity of provincial foods, the Cantina has won the distinguished *Travel/Holiday* and *Washingtonian Magazine* awards for the fourteen years it has been open. Moreover, the restaurant has received high ratings in American, French, and Swiss travel guides.

Today, Joseph continues to derive his ideas from reading and travel, at one point tracing the origins of a dish to Roman antiquity. Necessarily, the menu changes at least once a week to accommodate new additions to the fare.

1214A - 18th Street, N.W.

RISOTTO BAROLO

5 tablespoons unsalted butter
1 medium-size yellow onion,
   finely diced
1½ cups arborio rice
1 cup SEASONED CHICKEN
   BROTH (see next page)

1 bottle Piemontèis Barolo
   wine
1 cup freshly grated Italian
   Parmesan cheese

1. In a 10-inch sauté pan, melt 4 tablespoons of the butter over medium heat. Add the onion and sauté until golden brown. Add the rice and the Seasoned Chicken Broth, stirring constantly with a wooden spoon to prevent sticking.
2. When the rice has absorbed the broth, add 3 cups of the wine. Stirring constantly, continue to cook about 25 to 30 minutes until the rice is tender. The rice may require a little more wine as it cooks to achieve the desired moistness.
3. Stir in the remaining butter and the Parmesan. Serve in six deep bowls or small plates.

It is important to use only the arborio rice from Italy, available at all Italian groceries as well as many food markets. In the Piemonte, Val d'Aosta and other regions of northern Italy, rice replaces pasta as a first course. The Barolo with its special flavor makes this first course unique.

CANTINA D'ITALIA

SEASONED CHICKEN BROTH

1 (5-pound) stewing hen
3 to 4 pounds chicken scraps
and bones
2 carrots, peeled and chopped
1 medium-size yellow onion,
peeled and quartered
2 stalks celery, washed
½ green or red pepper, chopped

2 tomatoes, peeled, seeded,
and chopped (canned
tomatoes optional)
1 small potato, peeled and
quartered
1 teaspoon salt
Pinch of tarragon

1. Place all the ingredients in a large stockpot and cover with at least 2 quarts cold water. Do not cover. Place over moderate heat and bring to a full boil. Reduce heat so that liquid just simmers.

2. Remove any scum that appears on the surface. Cover the pot and cook 3 to 4 hours.

3. Using a fine sieve lined with dampened cheesecloth, strain the mixture into a clean pot or large bowl.

4. Let the broth cool well, then refrigerate. Remove the congealed fat from the surface. Reheat as needed, freezing the unused portion for future use.

ZUPPA MINESTRA DI POMODORI

1 pound ripe tomatoes
1 clove garlic, halved
8 leaves fresh basil, washed
1 teaspoon salt
1 tablespoon fresh lemon juice
1 teaspoon grated nutmeg
2 tablespoons unsalted butter

2 tablespoons flour
4 cups SEASONED CHICKEN
    BROTH
1 tablespoon sugar (optional)
    Sliced Italian bread, toasted
    and rubbed with garlic

1. Peel and coarsely chop the tomatoes, saving the juice. In a deep, heavy saucepan, combine the tomatoes and juice with the garlic, basil, salt, lemon juice, and nutmeg. Bring to a full boil. Lower heat and simmer gently approximately 30 minutes. Cool and purée in an electric blender.

2. Rinse the saucepan and dry well. Place over medium heat and melt the butter. Blend in the flour, stirring vigorously about 1 minute. Add the Seasoned Chicken Broth, stirring constantly with a large wooden spoon until the mixture comes to a full boil. Cover and cook over low heat about 12 minutes.

3. Add the tomato purée to the thickened broth and cook over low heat approximately 15 minutes longer. Taste and add the sugar, if the broth seems too acid. Serve hot in bowls or chill well and serve cold. If desired, float the slices of Italian bread on top.

This is a very light soup served in Torino. I have always believed that soup should never be overlooked in a meal, but that it also should never be filling. Substitute canned Italian plum tomatoes if good, ripe tomatoes are not available.

INSALATA DI CÀVOLO ROSSO CON BAGNA CAUDA

1 *large head red cabbage*
1 *cup BAGNA CAUDA ALLA*
TORINO

5 *tablespoons red wine*
vinegar

1. Quarter and core the cabbage, discarding any bruised outer leaves. Shred coarsely into long, thin slices. Place in a deep bowl and fill with cold water to allow grit to settle. Remove carefully and drain well or spin dry.
2. Place the shredded cabbage in a large salad bowl. Add the hot Bagna Cauda and vinegar. Toss well. Serve hot or chilled.

Note: The Bagna Cauda must be hot when tossed with the cabbage.

BAGNA CAUDA ALLA TORINO

1 *cup good-quality imported*
olive oil
16 *cloves garlic, crushed*

2 *(2-ounce) cans anchovy*
fillets
1 *cup whipping cream*

1. Heat the oil in a small, deep saucepan. Add the garlic and anchovy fillets, stirring constantly for about 5 minutes. Use a wooden spoon to mash the fillets aginst the side of the pan. The fillets should almost melt in the hot oil.
2. Slowly add the cream, stirring constantly. Lower heat and simmer at least 30 minutes, stirring frequently. Do not add salt.

This sauce is very popular in Piemonte, where the name means "hot bath" in the Piemontèis dialect. Try serving as a dip with assorted fresh vegetables and Italian bread. To vary the taste and texture of the cabbage salad, replace the cream with 1½ cups of Barbera d'Alba, a dry red wine from Alba.

COSTOLETTE ALLA VALDOSTANA

½ pound Val d' Aosta
  fontina cheese
6 (1"-thick) veal chops
  Salt and pepper
2½ tablespoons all-purpose
  flour
1 egg, well beaten

½ cup fine dry bread
  crumbs
¼ pound unsalted butter
3 lemons, cut in wedges
  Parsley sprigs (optional)

1. Slice the cheese thinly. Cut a slit into the side of each veal chop to form a pocket. Stuff the pockets with the cheese.
2. Place the chops on a flat surface and press the top and bottom together. Seal the edges by beating hard with a heavy knife or mallet. Season lightly with the salt and pepper.
3. Dredge the chops in the flour, dip in the beaten egg, and coat with the bread crumbs. Melt the butter in a heavy skillet or sauté pan. Add the chops and sauté about 15 minutes or until golden brown on both sides.
4. Serve piping hot, surrounded by the lemon wedges and garnished, if desired, with a few parsley sprigs.

For this dish, you must obtain Val d'Aosta fontina. The Swiss variety will not be the same. Cooking is like most other things in life, you know. You have to go to a little extra effort. Nothing is just simply handed to you. This recipe requires such effort, but for you it always will be a worthy accomplishment.

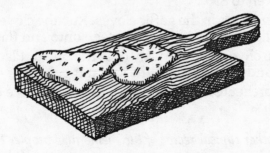

SPINACI ALLA PIEMONTÈIS

3 pounds fresh spinach
Pinch of salt
¾ cup unsalted butter

6 to 8 anchovy fillets, finely diced
2 cloves garlic, finely minced
Pepper

1. Wash the spinach several times in very cold water to remove grit. Do not dry. Pile into a deep saucepan and add the salt. Cover and place over medium heat and cook about 4 minutes until spinach is tender. Do not overcook.
2. Drain well, then squeeze the cooked spinach dry. In a large skillet, melt the butter until it just begins to turn brown. Add the anchovies, garlic, a little pepper, and the spinach. Reduce heat to low at once. Sauté together 5 minutes, stirring constantly. Serve at once, piping hot.

Don't be surprised to find that your spinach has shrunk terribly after the first step in this recipe. That is the way with spinach. This dish has a robust flavor and offers a good color contrast to the veal. The two dishes make a perfect pair.

SOMA D'AI
Piemontèis Garlic Bread

6 cloves garlic
Large loaf of Italian bread

Italian olive oil
Salt and pepper

1. Preheat oven to 350°.
2. Make several cuts in the garlic cloves. Rub the cloves over the Italian bread to allow the garlic juices to seep onto and flavor the crust.
3. Spread the olive oil generously over the bread. Place on a large baking sheet and sprinkle with the salt and pepper.
4. Warm in preheated oven about 10 minutes. Serve directly from the oven.

This is another typical recipe of the Piemontèis people. Here at the Cantina we serve it either at room temperature or oven-warmed. It is excellent with a fish soup or stew.

CROSTINI ALL'AGLIO E MOZZARELLA
Garlic Bread with Mozzarella

12 thick slices Italian bread	½ cup unsalted butter, at room temperature
3 cloves garlic, finely crushed	
2 cups diced whole-milk mozzarella (about 1 pound)	½ cup chopped fresh basil leaves
1 cup good-quality Italian olive oil	2 teaspoons tomato paste Salt and pepper

1. Preheat oven to 425°. Lay the bread slices on large baking sheets.
2. Place the garlic in a deep bowl and add the cheese, olive oil, butter, basil, tomato paste, and the salt and pepper to taste.
3. Mix well together, then spread over each slice of bread. Place the bread slices in the hot oven and bake until the cheese melts. Serve at once.

These are two totally different types of garlic bread. When served together in a napkin-lined bread basket, they offer the diner a veritable feast! I enjoy this, myself, with a big salad or just a bowl of clear broth. In this recipe, be sure to use the salt sparingly; the flavors are good without too much added.

ZABAGLIONE

6 large egg yolks	6 tablespoons sweet Marsala wine
2 tablespoons granulated sugar	

1. In the bottom half of a double boiler, bring about 2 inches of water to a simmer. It is most important that the water not be too hot, and that the top half not touch the water's surface.
2. Beat the egg yolks and sugar together in the top half, using a strong, balloon-type whisk.
3. Slowly add the Marsala to the egg mixture, continuing to beat about 4 to 6 minutes until the custard becomes thick and fluffy. Pile into long-stemmed glasses and serve at once.

This particular type of Italian pudding should always be served hot. You must use great caution to see to it that the water does not come in contact with the egg yolk mixture, or you will have scrambled sweet eggs. Other than that, it is very easy.

Dinner for Six

Hot Buttered Brie

Spinach, Bacon, and Mushroom Salad with House Dressing

Filet Béarnaise

Broiled Tomatoes

Cottage Fries

Fresh Fruit Omelette Soufflé

Cappuccino l'Amore

Wines:

With the Brie—Muscadet, Marquis de Goulaine, Loire, 1979

With the Filet—Côte Rôtie, Domaine Gerin, Rhône, 1973

With the Soufflé—Domaine Chandon Blanc de Noir

John Laythan and Stuart C. Davidson, Owners

Jacob Gravitt, Chef

CLYDE'S

In 1963, a motorcycle saloon on M Street in Georgetown was converted to what has become a household name in Washington, D.C., for great fun and great food—Clyde's restaurant. With a menu that ranges from special burgers and omelettes to steak and seafood entrées, with an atmosphere that is at once both relaxed and upbeat, Clyde's is a place to meet, feast, and celebrate.

Heavily etched glass double doors lead the way inside where numerous lively signs and posters paper the dark wood-panelled walls. At Clyde's, a patron has the choice of three different dining areas in which to enjoy himself and the background. In the main rooms, where a long, heavy wooden bar forms a focal point, the tables are spread with bright red-checked tablecloths. Omelettes are featured in what is called, not surprisingly, the Omelette Room, where the tablecloths are yellow and white-checked. And the blue-checked tablecloths in the flower-filled Atrium reflect the light of a huge skylight, providing the guests with the illusion of dining outdoors.

To have been trained in the Omelette Room at Clyde's is quite a credit for a chef because this specialty is prepared with such style, such flair, that it takes months to learn the technique. Happily, it takes little study for a diner to learn to enjoy such outstanding delicacies as the Bonne Femme, an omelette filled with bacon, sautéed potatoes, and onions, laced with sour cream and chives, or the Normandy, made with sautéed mushrooms and herb cheese.

So popular did this restaurant quickly become that it has branched out to two new spots: a waterside café in Columbia, Maryland, and a lush, luxurious setting in Tyson's Corner, Virginia. Whether one desires a complete meal, a late afternoon drink and one of the "Afternoon Delights" to whet the appetite, or a sweet midnight snack, be sure to visit the eclectic and always energetic Clyde's.

3236 M Street, N.W.

HOT BUTTERED BRIE

½ cup sliced almonds
1 (½-pound) wheel Brie
cheese

¼ pound unsalted butter,
sliced into 8 pieces
Large loaf of French bread

1. Preheat oven to 325°.
2. Spread the almonds on a sheet of aluminum foil and then place in preheated oven about 5 minutes or until lightly browned. Watch carefully and stir once or twice so that they toast evenly. Remove the almonds and increase oven temperature to 350°.
3. Place the wheel of Brie in an ovenproof serving dish. Sprinkle with the toasted almonds, then top with the slices of butter. Bake 20 to 30 minutes. The Brie should look puffy and be rather jelly-like to the touch when it is ready.
4. Slice the French bread into ¼-inch slices and arrange in a napkin-lined basket. Cover with foil to keep fresh until time to serve.
5. Place the dish containing the hot Brie on a chafing dish and serve with the basket of bread, letting guests dip the bread slices into the melted brie.

At all our locations, this is our most popular appetizer. The almonds can be toasted ahead of time.

SPINACH, BACON, AND MUSHROOM SALAD
WITH HOUSE DRESSING

2 pounds fresh spinach
12 slices bacon
1 pound mushrooms,
    washed and dried

Lemon juice
LEMON-OIL HOUSE
  DRESSING

1. Preheat oven to 350°.
2. Wash the spinach leaves several times in cold water, allowing grit to settle. Spin or towel dry, then place in a bowl and refrigerate.
3. Lay bacon on a baking sheet and bake slowly in preheated oven until well done. Drain on paper towels. Crumble the cooled bacon into bite-size pieces and reserve.
4. Slice the mushrooms. Sprinkle with the lemon juice and refrigerate until ready to use.
5. Place the spinach, mushrooms, and bacon in a large salad bowl. Pour half the Lemon-Oil House Dressing over the vegetables and mix lightly. Pour the rest into a gravy boat. Serve at once.

LEMON-OIL HOUSE DRESSING

1 egg yolk
2 tablespoons Dijon
    mustard
1 teaspoon pressed fresh
    garlic

½ teaspoon salt
½ teaspoon white pepper
1½ cups salad oil
2 tablespoons fresh lemon
    juice

1. Briefly whisk the egg yolk in a small mixing bowl. Add the mustard, garlic, salt, and pepper and mix thoroughly.
2. Whisk in ½ cup of the oil in a steady stream, followed by half the lemon juice.
3. Repeat with another ½ cup of the oil, followed by the rest of the lemon juice.
4. Whisk in the remaining ½ cup oil and whisk all together for 1 or 2 minutes.

This dressing has become so popular that we have begun bottling it and selling it through one of the local grocery stores. Combined with the spinach, bacon, and mushroom salad, it is excellent.

CLYDE'S

FILET BÉARNAISE

6 *English muffins*	*Salt and pepper*
12 *(¾"-thick) slices filet*	*BÉARNAISE SAUCE (see*
mignon (about 2 pounds)	*next page)*

1. Preheat broiler.
2. Carefully split the English muffins with a fork. Set aside.
3. Broil the filets about 2 to 6 minutes on each side, or until done to taste. Season very lightly with the salt and pepper. Toast the muffin halves. Top each with a filet, then place the two halves on each of six warmed plates. Cover liberally with the warm Béarnaise Sauce. Serve at once with Broiled Tomatoes and Cottage Fries.

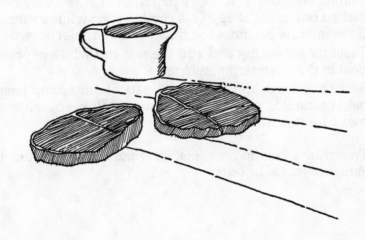

CLYDE'S

BÉARNAISE SAUCE

½ cup white wine vinegar
½ cup dry white wine
2 tablespoons shallots, finely chopped
Salt and white pepper
1 tablespoon dried tarragon
6 egg yolks

¾ pound butter, melted
¼ cup fresh tarragon, washed and finely diced (approximately)
1 tablespoon butter, at room temperature (optional)

1. Place the vinegar, wine, shallots, ¼ teaspoon pepper, a pinch of salt, and the dried tarragon in a small saucepan. Place over medium-high heat and bring to a full boil. Boil until the liquid is reduced to one-fourth its original volume. Remove from heat and cool.
2. Place the egg yolks in the top of a double boiler over simmering water. Beat with a heavy whisk to the consistency of mayonnaise.
3. Using a fine sieve, strain the cooled vinegar mixture into the eggs, beating vigorously. Remove pan from heat and very slowly add the melted butter to the egg yolk combination while continuing to beat. If the mixture becomes too thick, add a droplet or two of water.
4. Taste for seasoning and add the salt and white pepper as needed. Beat in the fresh tarragon to taste.
5. Serve at once or top with 1 or 2 pats of butter and keep warm in a bain-marie. Do not cover. The sauce will keep in a very low bain-marie for hours.

Presenting a beautiful combination of textures and flavors, this platter is American food at its best!

BROILED TOMATOES

3 *large, fresh, ripe*
   tomatoes

6 *tablespoons freshly grated*
   Parmesan cheese

1. Preheat oven to 350°. Slice each tomato in half. Place the halves on a baking sheet and sprinkle each with a tablespoon of the Parmesan.
2. Place tomatoes in preheated oven and bake about 15 minutes. The tomatoes should be cooked but still firm. Remove and turn oven to broil.
3. Watching carefully, brown the tops of the tomatoes under the broiler. Remove and serve at once.

COTTAGE FRIES

6 *large Idaho potatoes,*
   peeled

Peanut oil
Salt

1. Slice the potatoes horizontally in thick slices. Rinse three times in cold water to remove starch. Pat dry with a linen towel and keep covered.
2. Pour the oil in a deep-fryer to a depth of 4 or 5 inches and heat to 400°, using a deep-fat thermometer. Place half the sliced potatoes in the fryer basket and lower into the hot oil. Cook until golden brown, then drain in a pan lined with paper towels.
3. Sprinkle immediately with salt.
4. Fry the remaining potato slices and serve at once.

CLYDE'S

FRESH FRUIT OMELETTE SOUFFLÉ

1 cup plus 2 tablespoons sugar
6 tablespoons egg whites (about 3)
Salt
⅛ teaspoon cream of tartar
¾ teaspoon vanilla extract
6 eggs
2 tablespoons whipping cream

2 tablespoons butter, at room temperature
2 tablespoons brown sugar
2 ounces cream cheese, thinly sliced
1 cup fresh strawberries, washed and sliced
Confectioners' sugar

1. Place 1 cup sugar, ⅓ cup water, and a candy thermometer in a heavy saucepan. Bring to a boil over medium-high heat and cook, swirling the mixture occasionally with the handle of the pot to keep sugar crystals from forming on the sides of the pan. Do not use a utensil.

2. Using an electric beater, beat the egg whites in a deep bowl until they form soft peaks. Add a scant pinch of salt and the cream of tartar, then beat vigorously until the egg whites are stiff. Add ¼ teaspoon of the vanilla and mix.

3. When the syrup has reached the soft ball stage, about 230°, add one drop at a time to the egg whites, beating constantly. Beat until all the hot syrup is incorporated into the egg whites. Continue to beat about 10 minutes until the meringue is cooled and very thick and stiff. Refrigerate until ready to use.

4. Combine the eggs, remaining 2 tablespoons sugar, cream, remaining ½ teaspoon vanilla, and a pinch of salt in a large bowl. Whisk together very well.

5. Gently combine the meringue into the sweet egg mixture. The meringue need not be completely incorporated.

6. Preheat broiler. Place a 12-inch omelette pan on the stove over barely moderate heat. Add the butter and melt. Be sure to coat the pan completely with the butter. Pour in the soufflé mixture. Use a fork to move the mixture around the pan in a circular motion while moving the pan back and forth across the burner.

46

7. When the omelette soufflé begins to rise, sprinkle the top with the brown sugar and place the slices of cream cheese across the center. Place under the broiler so that the top can brown. Do not burn. Remove.

8. Fold the omelette soufflé in half in the pan then slide onto a medium-size platter. Spoon on the strawberries and dust well with the confectioners' sugar. Slice at the table into six wedges.

Note: Both the meringue and the sweet egg mixture can be prepared in advance and stored, covered, in the refrigerator.

Susie Thompson created this dish when she opened our Omelette Room in 1973. For variety, you can prepare a chocolate omelette by adding chocolate sauce to the sweet egg mixture, or you can flambé the soufflé on the platter with heated Grand Marnier.

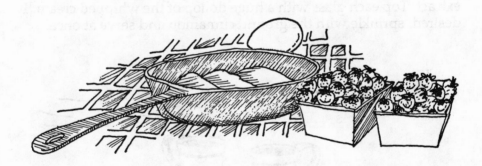

CAPPUCCINO L'AMORE

5 ounces gin
5 ounces rum
5 ounces brandy
10 ounces crème de cacao
2½ ounces Galliano
12 whole cloves
4 whole cinnamon sticks

CAPPUCCINO
1 cup whipping cream
3 tablespoons sifted confectioners' sugar
1 drop vanilla extract
Ground cinnamon
(optional)

1. Combine the first 7 ingredients in a quart jar. Cover and let the spices steep in the liqueurs for 48 hours.
2. Strain through cheesecloth into a clean jar and store in the refrigerator until ready to use.
3. Pour 1½ ounces of the liqueur mixture into the bottom of each of six 8-ounce glasses. Fill almost to the top with the hot Cappuccino.
4. Beat the cream with the confectioners' sugar and mix in the vanilla extract. Top each glass with a huge dollop of the whipped cream. If desired, sprinkle with the ground cinnamon and serve at once.

CLYDE'S

CAPPUCCINO

2 cups freshly brewed
espresso coffee
2⅔ cups half and half, hot

2 tablespoons unsweetened
cocoa
1⅓ cups sugar
3 shakes ground cinnamon

Combine the hot espresso with the rest of the ingredients.

This is a favorite at Clyde's, and, for many years, was a well-kept secret. One of the problems in giving the recipe was that we always made it in such large quantities; it was almost impossible to break it down. But at last we have it, and here it is.

Dominique's

Dinner for Four

Salmon Fricassee

Rattlesnake Salad

Quails in Batter

Fresh Spinach Salad with Raspberry Vinaigrette and Goat's Cheese

Chocolate Truffles

Wines:

Before dinner—Champagne, Moët et Chandon White Label

With the Salmon—Chassagne-Montrachet, Louis Latour, 1979

With the Quail—Châteauneuf-du-Pape,
Domaine de Mont Redon, 1978

Dominique D'Ermo, Owner

Alain Binot, Executive Chef

Diana Damewood, General Manager

Dominique's, the namesake of proprietor Dominique D'Ermo, is a French restaurant unlike any other, as was expressly intended. Dominique discovered through years of travel that French restaurants worldwide regrettably have two things in common: a map of France adorning one of the walls, and the same menu, with price the only variant. Although a cartographer's handiwork does adorn a wall of this restaurant, and although some dishes are decidedly French, at Dominique's a patron can enjoy so much more—and leave so much more satisfied.

Dominique emigrated from France when he was twenty-eight years old and arrived in the United States with only ten dollars in his pocket. Working as the pastry chef for the Americana Hotel in Miami Beach, as well as in various capacities for Prince Hotels International and the Shoreham Hotel in Washington, D.C., provided him with the resources to open his own restaurant. He is very visible there, eager to help his guests make selections or to meet any of their desires. The philosophy by which he operates his establishment is that "we never say no to a customer." So far, he has managed to fulfill each and every request.

While all of the dishes he serves are superb, some of the best are those that cannot even be found elsewhere, such as Baby Mallard Duck braised in Poivrade Sauce and served with kiwi fruit, fresh mushrooms, and red cabbage. An indication of Dominique's dedication to his art is that, whenever possible, guests are served meat from animals which he himself hunts. Some other offerings, like the recipe for Rattlesnake Salad included here, have been known to be somewhat controversial, yet equally exciting and inimitable.

Most of the restaurant's furnishings, many of which Dominique secured, suggest a rural French mood—a huge pot rack filled with hammered pots, for example, or the country stove functioning as the reservations desk. But the etched glass dividers, bronze busts, and heavy tapestries give the impression, instead, of a turn-of-the-century Parisian restaurant. This eclectic decor, combined with the din emanating from the always crowded tables against a background of accordian music, makes Dominque's fine, fun, and unforgettable.

20th & Pennsylvania Avenue, N.W.

SALMON FRICASSEE

1 pound boneless fresh salmon Salt and pepper	½ cup dry white wine
1 teaspoon dry mustard	1 tablespoon chopped fresh chives
⅓ cup wine vinegar	1 tablespoon chopped fresh parsley
1 tablespoon finely chopped fresh shallots	3 large ripe tomatoes, peeled and seeded
1 tablespoon finely chopped fresh garlic	4 tablespoons unsalted butter

1. Cut the salmon into pieces approximately 1-inch square and sprinkle lightly with salt and pepper. Place in a deep saucepan.
2. In a small bowl, mix together the mustard and vinegar and pour over the fish. Add the remaining ingredients to the saucepan and bring to a boil.
3. Reduce heat and simmer gently for 10 minutes or until the salmon is just tender. Serve hot.

Note: Mako shark or swordfish may be substituted for the salmon.

Here at Dominique's, we serve the fricassee in soup bowls mounded with dollops of mashed potatoes. Lift the potatoes into peaks so that they look like little white mountains surrounded by the pink broth. If the appetizer is served this way, a separate starch dish is not needed in the menu.

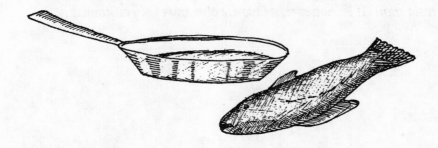

DOMINIQUE'S

RATTLESNAKE SALAD

4 pounds rattlesnake,
  skinned and cleaned, head
  and tail removed
2 cups dry white wine
2 cups water
  Bouquet garni:
    1 sprig thyme
    1 bay leaf
    6 sprigs parsley
  Salt and pepper

½ cup diced celery
⅓ cup diced Spanish onions
  Juice of 1 lemon
1 tablespoon Dijon mustard
¼ cup chopped fresh parsley
¼ to ½ cup mayonnaise
1 head lettuce
12 fresh radishes
1 lemon, cut into wedges
  Capers

1. Cut the snake into 12-inch pieces and place in a saucepan. Pour the wine and water over the snake. Add the bouquet garni and sprinkle with salt and pepper.

2. Cover the pan tightly and bring to a boil. Reduce heat and simmer about 15 minutes, or until the meat tests tender when pierced with the tongs of a large meat fork. Bone the meat.

3. Place the meat in a deep, round bowl and add the celery, onion, lemon juice, and mustard. Season with salt and pepper. Add the parsley. Gradually blend in mayonnaise to duplicate the consistency of tuna fish salad.

4. Make a bed of lettuce on four salad plates. Serve the salad on the beds of lettuce and garnish with the radishes, 1 lemon wedge, and capers.

This is the dish that has brought so much controversy and notoriety to my restaurant. It is, however, a favorite of many of my customers.

QUAILS IN BATTER

8 quails, cleaned and split
in half lengthwise
6 tablespoons all-purpose
flour
Salt and pepper
4 eggs, lightly beaten
1 cup fresh white bread
crumbs

⅓ cup butter
¼ cup finely chopped fresh
parsley
Juice of 1 lemon
SAUTÉED APPLE SLICES
or FRIED GRAPES (see
next page)

1. Lay the quail halves on a flat surface and press each firmly to flatten slightly.
2. Dredge the quail in the flour, sprinkle with salt and pepper, and dip in the beaten eggs. Roll the quail in the bread crumbs and set aside.
3. Melt the butter in a deep saucepan or large sauté pan. When the butter is sizzling, add the quail halves and cook for 5 minutes on each side. If the pan cannot accommodate all at one time, cook in two batches.
4. Sprinkle with the parsley and add the lemon juice. Cover the pan and simmer 5 minutes longer. Serve immediately, surrounded by the Sautéed Apple Slices or Fried Grapes.

This unusual and excellent preparation is a famous French specialty. When served, Quails in Batter appears to be much more difficult to prepare than it really is.

SAUTÉED APPLE SLICES

4 firm apples (preferably
    Granny Smith or Golden
    Delicious)

3 tablespoons butter
Cinnamon
Nutmeg

1. Core the apples and slice into circles. Do not peel.
2. Melt the butter in a sauté pan. When the butter foams, add the apple slices. Sauté 3 to 4 minutes until golden. While sautéing, lift the slices carefully with a wide spatula to prevent them from breaking.
3. Sprinkle with the nutmeg and cinnamon.

FRIED GRAPES

2 cups seedless green grapes
½ cup all-purpose flour
2 eggs, beaten

1 cup fresh bread crumbs
Vegetable oil
Paprika (optional)

1. Rinse the grapes thoroughly under cool water, separating the stems. Do not dry. Roll in the flour, then dip in the eggs. Toss in the bread crumbs, coating evenly. Place the coated grapes on an uncovered platter and refrigerate 1 hour before frying. This will make the breading adhere well.
2. Heat the oil to 375°. Drop the grapes into the hot oil and deep-fry about 12 seconds.
3. Remove the grapes with a slotted spoon and drain on paper towels. Sprinkle with the paprika before serving, if desired.

FRESH SPINACH SALAD WITH RASPBERRY VINAIGRETTE AND GOAT'S CHEESE

¾ pound fresh spinach,
　stems removed
¼ cup raspberry vinegar
2 tablespoons Dijon mustard
1 teaspoon salt
¼ teaspoon freshly ground
　black pepper

1 clove fresh garlic,
　crushed
2 tablespoons water
¾ cup olive oil
2 ounces goat's cheese,
　crumbled

1. Wash the spinach in cold water many times, draining well after each washing. Spin dry and refrigerate, or place in refrigerator on several paper towels to dry.
2. In a deep bowl, whisk the vinegar, mustard, salt, pepper, crushed garlic, and water together until the salt dissolves. Slowly add the oil, blending with the whisk until the dressing thickens slightly. Add the crumbled goat's cheese and mix with a small spoon.
3. Pile the spinach leaves on four salad plates. Pour the dressing over each, dividing the bits of cheese evenly so that little bits of the white fleck the dark green leaves.

This is an excellent salad, one that will serve as a complete change from the previous courses, yet prepare you for the grand dessert to follow.

CHOCOLATE TRUFFLES

10 ounces semisweet chocolate
1 pint whipping cream
4 tablespoons unsalted
   butter
2 tablespoons granulated
   sugar
4 tablespoons Grand Marnier

½ cup sifted confectioners'
   sugar
6 ounces sweet chocolate
½ cup plus 1 tablespoon unsweetened cocoa powder
⅓ cup sliced roasted almonds

1. Grate the semisweet chocolate and place in the top of a double boiler over hot water. Melt slowly on low heat, taking care that the chocolate does not burn.

2. Place 1 cup of the cream, the butter, and sugar in a heavy, deep saucepan and bring to a boil. Remove from heat and add the melted chocolate, blending well. Add the Grand Marnier and mix.

3. Place over a bowl of crushed ice and whip slowly until mixture cools and thickens. The chocolate should be the consistency of mashed potatoes.

4. Using a pastry bag or teaspoon, drop little balls of the chocolate about ½ inch apart on cookie sheets lined with parchment or waxed paper. Balls should be the size of cherry tomatoes. Freeze about four hours to harden.

5. Remove the truffles from freezer and dust heavily with the confectioners' sugar. Roll each in the palm of the hand. Freeze about 1 hour to harden.

6. Grate the sweet chocolate and melt over warm water. As a dipping sauce, the chocolate should not go over 80° to 84°. Measure temperature with a candy thermometer.

7. Remove truffles from freezer and dip each in the melted chocolate. Freeze about 1 hour to harden.

8. Remove truffles from freezer. Warm to room temperature, then dust with the cocoa powder. Refrigerate. When ready to serve, whip 1 cup of cream. Place two truffles on each plate and top with plenty of whipped cream. Sprinkle with the almonds and serve.

This recipe yields about twenty-five truffles and can be doubled. Truffles will keep in the freezer about fifteen days.

Chocolate Truffle is a very special confection I devised for Elizabeth Taylor Warner. She is a lovely, gracious lady whose good taste is surpassed only by her beauty.

LE GAULOIS

Dinner for Four

Les Moules Persillées

Potage Borsch

Les Spaghettie de Courgettes des Pêcheurs

Salade Maison

Tia Maria Mousse

Wine:

Mâcon Chardonnay, Cooperative of Chardonnay, 1980

Dara and Bernard Baudrand, Owners

Bernard Baudrand, Executive Chef

LE GAULOIS

Owners Bernard and Dara Baudrand have created in Le Gaulois a French restaurant of some distinction. Unlike many French restaurants, it is not a solemn, formal establishment which caters largely to the tastes of the affluent. Instead, this café-like restaurant is a warm and happy place where people of all means can enjoy exquisite gourmet French food.

Bernard, the executive chef, brings first-class experience to his restaurant, having worked in the kitchen since he was fourteen years old and having served his chef apprenticeship in Paris. He is an outstanding and imaginative chef as the *Washingtonian Magazine* recognized when they nominated him to be one of three chefs considered for their Best Chef award. He carefully plans and often changes the menu to the delight of his clientele, but the quality never varies. Bernard will serve only the freshest of food, going so far as to bake the pastries on the premises twice daily, to insure that his guests can enjoy peak flavor.

The restaurant is warmly decorated. Copper pots hang on the wood-paneled walls; fresh flowers grace the tables which are placed close together in the European style. This positioning lends a friendly intimacy to the mood of the restaurant which is matched by the congenial manner of the waiters and waitresses. Le Gaulois had the honor to be named one of the ten best restaurants in the area by the *Washingtonian Magazine*, and it is a well-deserved credit. Few other restaurants can provide their guests with such a delicious feast, in such an amiable setting, and at such a reasonable cost.

2133 Pennsylvania Avenue, N.W.

LES MOULES PERSILLÉES
Mussels with Parsley and Garlic Butter

60 fresh mussels
1 cup chopped onion
1 cup white wine
3 shallots, chopped
 Freshly ground white
  pepper

Juice of 3 lemons
GARLIC PARSLEY BUTTER
 (see next page)
Chopped parsley (optional)

1. Scrub the mussels well under running water, discarding any that are already opened.
2. In a deep pot with a tight-fitting lid, place the onion, wine, shallots, and pepper and bring to a full boil over high heat. Add the mussels, cover, and steam 10 minutes over high heat.
3. Remove lid and drain the mussels, reserving the broth. Discard any mussels that have not opened. Remove the upper shells. Place the lower shells containing the meats in a shallow pan or bowl. Cover the mussels with some of the broth to prevent drying out, if not intending to use at once.
4. Preheat oven to 475°. Remove shells from pan or bowl and arrange on a large baking pan. Sprinkle with the lemon juice.
5. Spread about ½ teaspoon of the Garlic Parsley Butter on the top of each mussel. If desired, sprinkle sparingly with chopped parsley.
6. Bake in preheated oven 10 minutes. Pile fifteen piping hot mussels in each of four soup plates or escargot dishes. Serve at once.

It is of the utmost importance that you use fresh, first-class mussels. I order only the "cultured" variety. They are clean and there is less likelihood of any problem with bacteria. Of course, you still must use wisdom in judging whether to discard any before and after steaming.

Serve each dish of steaming mussels with chunks of crusty French bread to dunk into the melted garlic parsley butter.

LE GAULOIS

GARLIC PARSLEY BUTTER

3 cloves garlic

4 shallots

¾ pound plus 4 tablespoons
butter

¼ cup chopped parsley

3 tablespoons chives

2 anchovies

Freshly ground white
pepper

Using a blender or food processor, thoroughly blend all the ingredients. Chill until ready to use.

POTAGE BORSCH
Beef and Fresh Vegetable Soup with Sour Cream

2 pounds beef short ribs	3 Spanish onions, chopped
5 quarts Chicken Stock (see index)	¾ cup wine vinegar
½ head white cabbage	Salt and freshly ground white pepper
½ head red cabbage	1 (15-ounce) can beets with juice
2 large leeks, well-washed	1 pint sour cream
7 ounces smoked bacon, diced	Crusty French bread
¼ pound unsalted butter	

1. Trim most of the fat from the short ribs and place in a deep 8-quart stockpot. Cover with the chicken stock and bring to a full boil. Skim the scum from the surface and lower heat. Cover and simmer at least 1½ hours, or until the meat is very tender and nearly falling off the bones.

2. About 20 minutes before short ribs have finished cooking in the stock, wash the cabbages well and shred. Reserve. Slice the leeks into small circles and reserve.

3. Using a deep sauté pan, sauté the bacon until crisp and well-rendered. Spoon off the bacon fat, reserving about 1 tablespoon. Melt the butter in the pan with the bacon fat. Add the onions, leeks, and cabbage. Cover pan and sauté together about 5 minutes. Add the vinegar, cover, and steam 2 minutes longer.

4. Remove the short ribs from the stock. Dice the meat into small cubes and set aside. Strain the stock into the sauté pan and season with the salt and white pepper. Simmer about ½ hour.

5. Add the juice from the can of beets. Cook 15 minutes longer. Julienne the beets and add with the diced meat to the soup. Let the soup get very hot.

6. Ladle the steaming soup into warmed soup bowls, accompanied by ramekins of the sour cream and the bread.

By serving the sour cream separately, you allow each guest to put in the amount he or she wishes. Be sure to serve with lots of good, crusty bread. Refrigerate any soup left over. It is wonderful the second and even the third day.

LES SPAGHETTIE DE COURGETTES DES PECHEURS
Zucchini with Seafood in Cream

2 fresh tomatoes	2 cups whipping cream
1 (4 to 5-ounce) zucchini, washed well	½ cup lump crabmeat
4 tablespoons clarified butter	24 mussels, steamed open and shelled
1 tablespoon minced shallots	*BEURRE MANIÉ*
20 bay scallops	¼ cup fresh lemon juice
32 frozen baby shrimp, thawed, peeled, and deveined	Salt and freshly ground pepper
3 tablespoons dry vermouth	

1. Peel, seed, and dice the tomatoes in ⅓-inch pieces to yield 1 cup. Set aside. Using a mandoline, slice the zucchini lengthwise in strips ¼-inch wide. The strips of zucchini should resemble spaghetti.

2. Melt the clarified butter in a large sauté pan and cook the zucchini and shallots 30 seconds over high heat. Push the mixture to one side of the pan and add the scallops and shrimp. Cook 1 minute, turning the seafood once or twice.

3. Add the vermouth, diced tomatoes, and cream and bring to a full boil. Reduce heat and cook 30 seconds.

4. Using a skimmer, remove the zucchini, seafood, and tomato to a heated serving platter. Top these with the crabmeat and the steamed mussels.

5. Return the pan with the cream mixture to high heat and boil rapidly for 1 minute. Whisk in the Beurre Manié to thicken. Add the lemon juice and the salt and pepper to taste.

6. Pour the hot sauce over the platter filled with zucchini and seafoods and serve immediately.

I am frankly proud of this dish which I developed here at Le Gaulois. It has been featured in magazines around the country and has made our restaurant very well known.

BEURRE MANIÉ

1 *tablespoon butter, softened*	1 *tablespoon all-purpose flour*

Blend the butter and the flour together with a large spoon. Use as a thickener for sauces.

SALADE MAISON

1 *head Boston lettuce*	¼ *cup julienned beets or*
½ *head escarole*	*cooked fine string beans*
½ *bunch watercress*	*HOUSE DRESSING (see*
4 *large leaves romaine*	*next page)*
lettuce	*Chopped fresh parsley*
4 *slices tomato or 8 cherry*	
tomatoes	

1. Thoroughly wash and dry the Boston lettuce, escarole, watercress, and romaine lettuce. Keep chilled in a bowl covered with a damp paper towel or cloth.
2. Divide the greens evenly among four salad bowls. Top each with a tomato slice or 2 cherry tomatoes and the beets or string beans. Drizzle the salads with the House Dressing and sprinkle with the parsley. Serve at once with cruets of extra dressing.

Note: Use only the freshest greens and at least two of the varieties listed in the ingredients.

LE GAULOIS

HOUSE DRESSING

1 egg yolk
1 tablespoon Homemade
  Mayonnaise (see index)
2 tablespoons Dijon mustard
  (preferably Maille)
1 tablespoon chopped shallots
½ teaspoon chopped garlic

Juice of ½ lemon
⅛ to ¼ teaspoon freshly ground
  white pepper
1½ teaspoons salt
3 tablespoons red wine
  vinegar
1 cup cottonseed oil

1. Whisk together the egg yolk and the mayonnaise. Add all the remaining ingredients except the oil and mix together thoroughly.
2. Beat in the oil slowly and taste the seasoning. Add a little more salt and pepper, if desired.

Note: This recipe yields enough dressing for eight salads. Serve the extra dressing in cruets or refrigerate.

For variety, I often substitute other cooked vegetables for the beets or string beans which I favor most.

TIA MARIA MOUSSE

2 tablespoons instant Sanka
⅓ cup PASTRY CREAM,
  chilled
2 tablespoons sugar

¾ cup whipping cream,
  chilled
Tia Maria
Assorted fancy cookies

1. In a metal bowl, dissolve the instant coffee in 2 teaspoons warm water. Mix until smooth. Place over another bowl filled with ice.
2. Add the Pastry Cream and whisk until well blended. Add the sugar and the cream and whip until stiff. Keep cold over the ice.
3. Using a star tip fitted into a big pastry bag, pipe the mousse into dessert dishes or stemmed glasses and refrigerate.

4. Pour about 1 tablespoon Tia Maria over each serving of the mousse; then insert one or two of the cookies partially into each dish to form a pretty design. Serve at once.

You can prepare this mousse through step 3 the day before you serve it. It keeps well, refrigerated.

PASTRY CREAM

1⅓ cups plus ¼ cup cold milk	6 egg yolks
1 (2") piece vanilla bean, split	¼ cup all-purpose flour
½ cup sugar	Pinch of salt

1. In a heavy saucepan, combine 1⅓ cups milk and the vanilla; bring to a boil. While heating, beat the sugar and egg yolks together in a deep bowl.
2. Gradually add the flour and salt to the yolks, whisking well until completely blended. Pour the ¼ cup cold milk into the egg/flour mixture and mix. When the vanilla-flavored milk has boiled, remove the vanilla bean and pour into the egg mixture, whisking vigorously.
3. Strain the sauce back into the saucepan through a fine sieve or chinois. Cook, stirring constantly, until the mixture comes to a full boil. Boil for 2 minutes.
4. Remove from heat and cool, stirring from time to time to keep a film from forming on top. Cover and refrigerate.

Use extra pastry cream to fill Napoleons, wonderful Mocha Genoese, and many other confections.

GERMAINE'S

Dinner for Four

Crab Asparagus Soup

Cha Gio

Caramel Chicken

Seaweed Scallops

Chef's Mixed Oriental Vegetables

Squirrel Fish with Sweet and Sour Sauce

Beverages:

Chardonnay, Roudon-Smith, 1978

or

Tsing Tao (Chinese) or Singha (Thai) beer

Germaine and Dick Swanson, Owners

Germaine Swanson, Executive Chef

Germaine's is a restaurant as unique and exciting as the history of its staff. Having fled Hanoi for Saigon in 1954, Germaine, then a paratrooper nurse, met and wed a photographer for *Life* magazine, Dick Swanson. The day before the fall of the Saigon government in April, 1975, they and twelve members of Germaine's family escaped to Washington, D.C., where Germaine began to teach cooking classes. Her popularity grew quickly, and she was soon able to open a restaurant, able also to employ her foreign-born relatives. The unusual and exquisite restaurant which they have created has not gone unnoticed; it has received accolades from such worthy critics as *Gourmet* magazine and the *New York Times*.

The Pan-Asian menu at Germaine's features an overwhelming variety of cuisines—Indonesian, Japanese, Vietnamese, and Korean, just to mention a few. The courses include such specialties as Peking Pork with Eggplant, Thai Basil Beef, Japanese Beef, Shrimp Saigon Style, and Korean Shredded Beef. It is food prepared and served to pristine perfection as Germaine's uses absolutely no MSG or artificial food coloring. In addition, the chefs season each meal individually, requesting that each patron indicate how spicy he prefers his food.

Germaine's is a light and airy restaurant, decorated with plants and sunshine rather than heavy Oriental brocades. The brightness matches the mood of the clientele whose expectations for a special evening are always met when they dine at Germaine's.

2400 Wisconsin Avenue

GERMAINE'S

CRAB ASPARAGUS SOUP

2 quarts CHICKEN STOCK
1 (15-ounce) can white
   asparagus, cut in ½"
   pieces
½ pound fresh crabmeat
¼ teaspoon salt

White pepper
1 tablespoon cornstarch
1 egg white, lightly
   beaten
Chinese parsley,
   chopped

1. Combine the Chicken Stock and the asparagus in a saucepan and bring to a boil over high heat. Add the crabmeat, being certain it is free of all cartilage. Season with the salt and white pepper.

2. Reduce heat. Dissolve 1 tablespoon cornstarch in 2 tablespoons cold water. Add the dissolved cornstarch and the beaten egg white to the saucepan, stirring until the soup thickens slightly and the egg white congeals. Taste for seasoning and correct if necessary. Sprinkle with the parsley and serve steaming hot.

CHICKEN STOCK

4 to 5 pounds chicken backs
1 medium-size onion

1 (3") piece fresh gingerroot, lightly pounded

1. Wash the chicken backs in hot water and place in a 6 to 8-quart stockpot or marmite. Pour in 5 to 6 quarts water and add the onion and the ginger. Bring to a boil over high heat. Skim the surface of any foam or scum that rises to the top.

2. Reduce heat to low and simmer 4 hours, uncovered, until liquid is reduced by one-half. Remove chicken from stock and strain through a fine sieve into a large container. Cool. Cover and refrigerate overnight. Before using, skim off any congealed fat.

Make this stock the day before you intend to use it in the Crab Asparagus Soup.

CHA GIO
Vietnamese Spring Rolls

1 *pound fresh shrimp, or*	1 *cup grated carrots*
1 *(1-pound) can crabmeat*	1 *egg, beaten*
1 *cup cellophane noodles*	¼ *teaspoon salt (optional)*
1 *pound lean pork, ground*	½ *teaspoon black pepper*
½ *cup Chinese mushrooms,*	30 *(8") round sheets rice*
chopped	*paper, cut in half*
1 *cup fresh bean sprouts*	3 to 4 *cups vegetable oil*
1 *cup chopped onion*	

1. Shell, devein, and finely chop the shrimp, or drain the crabmeat and finely chop. Reserve. Place the cellophane noodles in a deep bowl, cover with cold water, and soak 15 minutes. Drain and cut into 1-inch strips.

2. In a large bowl, combine all the ingredients except the rice paper and the oil. Mix well and set aside.

3. Lay a half-sheet of the rice paper on a clean, flat surface and moisten well by dipping your fingers into a bowl of cold water, then wetting the paper thoroughly. Fold the rice paper in half and set aside to soften. Continue until all sheets are dampened. By the time the last is dampened, the first will be ready to fill.

4. Open the first sheet of dampened rice paper. Fill with 1 tablespoon of the shrimp/pork mixture. Roll the rice paper into a cylinder, tucking in the ends. Repeat, using the remaining sheets of rice paper.

5. Heat the wok until hot. Add the oil and heat to 375°. Reduce heat and allow oil to drop to 325°. Deep-fry the rolls until they are crisp and golden brown. Remove and drain well. Serve at once.

Serve spring rolls as a side dish or appetizer. If desired, fry the day before and reheat in a 400° oven for 5 minutes.

CARAMEL CHICKEN

4 whole chicken breasts	Vegetable oil
2 egg whites, lightly beaten	CARAMEL SAUCE
2 teaspoons water chestnut powder or cornstarch	1 teaspoon cornstarch
Dash of white pepper	1 large tomato, cut length- wise and sliced across into
1 teaspoon sesame seeds	thin slices for garnish

1. Preheat oven to 350°.
2. Skin the chicken breasts and remove the bones. Slice across the grain into ½ by 1-inch strips and set aside. Combine the beaten egg whites with the water chestnut powder or cornstarch and add the white pepper. Mix together with the chicken strips and marinate 20 minutes.
3. Put the sesame seeds into a small baking pan and place in preheated oven. Roast about 20 minutes, stirring often. Remove and set aside.
4. Pour 2 cups of the oil into a wok or deep-fryer and heat on high until about 350°. Deep-fry the chicken strips until golden, then transfer to a bowl.
5. Pour off all but 2 tablespoons of the oil and reheat. Add the Caramel Sauce and bring to a full boil. Dissolve 1 teaspoon cornstarch in 1 tablespoon cold water. Add to the sauce and cook until the sauce thickens. Add the chicken strips and mix well to coat completely.
6. Transfer to a platter and garnish with the sliced tomato. Top all with the roasted sesame seeds and serve at once.

Save the bones from the chicken breasts for your next pot of chicken stock.

CARAMEL SAUCE

3 tablespoons light soy sauce	3 tablespoons sugar
1 tablespoon mushroom sauce	1 tablespoon dry sherry
1 tablespoon Chinese black vinegar	½ teaspoon peeled, chopped fresh gingerroot
1 teaspoon chili paste (optional)	½ teaspoon chopped fresh garlic

Combine all ingredients.

SEAWEED SCALLOPS

2 cups vegetable oil
6 to 8 ounces fresh kale or collard
greens, washed, dried, and
shredded

1 pound scallops, washed,
dried, and sliced into ¼"
rounds
SAUCE

1. Pour the oil into a wok and heat to 375°. Add the greens and stir with a slotted spoon for 30 seconds. Drain well on a plate lined with paper towels. Arrange the cooked greens on a serving platter.
2. Reheat the oil, add the scallops, and cook about 30 seconds, or until they turn opaque. Transfer to a bowl and reserve.
3. Pour off all but 1 tablespoon of the oil. Lower heat and add the Sauce. Return heat to high and add the scallops. Stir-fry a few seconds in the sauce to coat evenly. Arrange the sauced scallops on the platter of fried greens and serve at once.

In resembling seaweed, fried greens not only contrast nicely with the Caramel Chicken, but also introduce a method of preparation unusual and unfamiliar to many Americans.

SAUCE

2 tablespoons soy sauce
2 tablespoons oyster sauce
1 tablespoon dry sherry
½ teaspoon chopped fresh
gingerroot

½ teaspoon chopped garlic
1 fresh hot red chili, finely
chopped
¼ teaspoon sugar

Combine the ingredients thoroughly in a small mixing bowl.

CHEF'S MIXED ORIENTAL VEGETABLES

2 to 3 *tablespoons vegetable oil*	1 *green or red sweet*
¼ *teaspoon chopped fresh*	*pepper, sliced*
gingerroot	4 to 5 *canned baby corn*
¼ *teaspoon chopped fresh*	½ *cup canned straw*
garlic	*mushrooms*
½ *medium-size onion, diced*	½ *cup CHICKEN STOCK*
1 *cup chopped Napa cabbage*	¼ *teaspoon sugar*
½ *cup snow peas*	1 *tablespoon soy sauce*
½ *cup sliced Chinese*	1 *tablespoon oyster sauce*
mushrooms	½ *teaspoon sesame oil*
½ *carrot, sliced or cut into*	*FRIED TOFU (optional)*
"flowers"	1 *teaspoon dry sherry*

1. Pour the oil into a wok and heat to 375°. Add the ginger, garlic, and onion. Stir-fry only 1½ minutes or until barely golden.
2. Add the cabbage, snow peas, Chinese mushrooms, carrot, pepper, baby corn, and straw mushrooms. Stir-fry 2 minutes. Add the Chicken Stock and cook for 2 minutes longer.
3. Add the sugar, soy sauce, oyster sauce, and sesame oil. Mix well. Add the Fried Tofu if desired and mix gently, being careful not to break up the tofu. Pour in the sherry and toss. Carefully transfer to a serving platter. Serve hot or at room temperature.

Orientals believe foods taste better if not served hot. Thus, many Oriental dishes are served at room temperature, a practice not customary in Western cooking.

FRIED TOFU

2 *cups vegetable oil*	½ *(4" to 5"-square) firm tofu*

1. Heat the oil in a wok or deep fryer to 375°. Carefully deep-fry the tofu until golden brown. Do not stir; the tofu must not break.
2. Using a large flat strainer, lift the fried tofu from the oil and place on a cutting surface. With a sharp knife, dice into 1-inch cubes and reserve.

SQUIRREL FISH WITH SWEET AND SOUR SAUCE

1 (3 to 4-pound) sea bass or
  rockfish
  Cornstarch
2 quarts soybean oil
2 tablespoons vegetable oil
⅓ teaspoon chopped garlic
⅓ teaspoon chopped fresh
  gingerroot
⅓ teaspoon chili paste

1½ cups CHICKEN STOCK
¼ cup sugar
¼ cup white vinegar
1 tablespoon soy sauce
¼ cup shredded carrot
¼ cup shredded snow peas
½ teaspoon sesame oil
STEAMED RICE

1. Using a sharp knife, cut the head off the fish and set aside. Cut the body almost in half by running the knife through the entire length of the belly from the base of the tail. Flatten slightly, then remove the backbone; be careful not to tear the skin. Score the flesh against the grain, then again on the diagonal. Cuts should be deep, almost to the skin, and three-fourths to one inch apart.

2. Dredge the scored fish body and the head in the cornstarch, coating evenly. Set aside.

3. Heat the soybean oil in a wok to 375°. Using tongs, hold the fish body by its tail and slip into the hot oil, skin side against the wok. While holding, cook the fish for 5 minutes, or until golden brown. Place on a serving platter and transfer to a warm oven. Add the head to the wok and cook about 3 minutes until golden brown. Keep warm in oven.

4. In a saucepan, combine the vegetable oil, garlic, ginger, chili paste, Chicken Stock, sugar, vinegar, and soy sauce. Bring to a boil over high heat.

5. Add the shredded carrot and snow peas. Lower heat. Dissolve 2 teaspoons of the cornstarch in 2 tablespoons cold water. Add the dissolved cornstarch and the sesame oil to the wok. Cook, stirring constantly, until sauce thickens.

6. Remove fish from oven. Pour the hot sauce over and serve at once with Steamed Rice.

GERMAINE'S

STEAMED RICE

2 cups Oriental long-
grain rice

3 cups cold water

1. Pour the rice into a fine strainer and wash several times. Drain and put into a 2½ to 3-quart saucepan with a tight-fitting lid. Add the cold water.
2. Place over high heat and bring to a full boil. Boil over medium heat until the water has evaporated. Reduce heat to very low, cover, and cook 10 to 15 minutes. Do not lift the lid.
3. Remove from heat; do not uncover. Let stand for 10 minutes. If not using immediately, place a damp linen towel under the lid and keep warm in a 150° to 175° oven, or keep barely warm over very low heat.

It is very important you use the specified rice and that you not disturb the lid once you have lowered the heat. Rice is very important in Oriental cooking and is an essential part of our day-to-day living. This recipe will not fail you.

GOLDEN PALACE

Dinner for Six

Golden Palace Special

Hard-Shell Crab with Black Bean Sauce and Green Onion

Seafood Soup with Bean Curd

Seafood Combination in Fried Taro Nest

Lamb with Ginger and Green Onions

Rainbow Chicken

Szechwan Pork with Shallots

Lichee Duck

Coconut Pudding with Fresh Fruits

Beverages:

With dinner—Tsing Tao beer

After dinner—hot tea

Nelson Lee, Owner and Executive Chef

GOLDEN PALACE

When Nelson Lee emigrated from Hong Kong some fifteen years ago, he was dismayed to discover that the "Chinese" food served in the United States was nothing like that at home. So he set about establishing the Golden Palace, a restaurant serving such exceptional Cantonese delicacies, with an ambiance so sophisticated and richly sensuous, that it has garnered much acclaim throughout Washington, D.C.

In the beginning, Nelson's dishes were so unusual that he had to persuade his patrons to sample new gastronomical delights by promising: "If you don't like it, you don't have to pay for it." It was an unnecessary bargain, however, because the care and attention lavished on all the restaurant's dishes—from Bird's Nest with Mashed Chicken Soup to Diced Chicken Malayian Style, from Kung Pao Lamb to Oyster with Scallion and Ginger Sauce—it all guaranteed a guest's satisfaction.

Over five years ago Nelson purchased what has become one of the Golden Palace's hallmarks, an enormous stove which allows gas-fed flames to shoot up from five huge openings and heat the kitchen's giant woks. Nelson could find no stove in America capable of such high heat, so he sent for one from Hong Kong. "You must have high heat to seal in the juices of your foods," he explains, "otherwise the foods become soggy and you end up with a mess." Not only does this magnificent contraption enable his conscientious and creative kitchen staff to cook each and every item to perfection, it also enables them to prepare twenty to thirty dishes for parties of as many as 200 individuals.

The Golden Palace is a luxurious restaurant. Heavily carved black screens provide privacy as well as elegance, as do the deep maroon colors of the furnishings, the tapestries, and the magnificent throne positioned in an alcove facing the entrance. The Golden Palace offers opulence and splendor to the connoisseur who insists on the best in service and Cantonese cuisine.

720–724 7th Street, N.W.

GOLDEN PALACE

GOLDEN PALACE SPECIAL

Per serving:

5 or 6 ice cubes	½ cup orange juice
¼ cup light rum	1 large, fresh orange slice
2 tablespoons banana liqueur	1 maraschino cherry, stemmed
2 tablespoons Myer's rum	
2 tablespoons Galliano	

1. Place the ice cubes in a cocktail shaker. Pour all the ingredients except the orange slice and cherry into the shaker and cover tightly. Shake vigorously. Remove top and pour into a tall, chilled glass.
2. Garnish with the orange slice, maraschino cherry, and an opened tiny Oriental parasol.

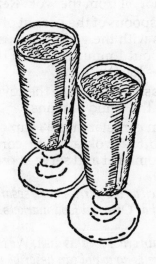

HARD -SHELL CRAB WITH BLACK BEAN SAUCE
AND GREEN ONION

6 fresh hard-shell crabs,
   shelled, cleaned, and cut
   in half through the middle
Cornstarch
Peanut oil
10 (¾") pieces green onion
   (about 3)

1 teaspoon garlic paste
1 teaspoon sesame oil
1 tablespoon black beans
   Dash of white pepper
⅓ cup rice wine
1¼ cups BASIC STOCK
   or water

1. Thoroughly coat the crab halves in the cornstarch. Pour peanut oil in a wok to about 5 inches in depth and heat until almost smoking. Add the crab and deep-fry for 1½ to 2 minutes, stirring often. Be sure to stir crab halves constantly in the hot oil, if they are to retain their juices and not become soggy. Deep-fry in two batches if necessary.

2. Remove immediately and place in a strainer set over a metal bowl to drain. Pour off the hot oil from the wok. Reheat wok.

3. Return about 2 tablespoons of the peanut oil to the hot wok and stir-fry the green onions with the garlic paste, sesame oil, black beans, and white pepper about 1 minute. Return the crabs to the wok and stir-fry 2 or 3 minutes longer.

4. Add the wine and Basic Stock, place the cover on the wok, and cook until about ¾ cup of the liquid remains.

5. Dissolve 1 teaspooon cornstarch in ¼ cup cold water. Add the dissolved cornstarch to the wok and stir constantly until the sauce thickens. Remove from heat and serve at once.

Special ingredients, such as the garlic paste, sesame oil, black beans, and rice wine, can be purchased at Oriental food markets.

I go far and wide to obtain crabs for this dish. We try to have fresh crabs available all year long. There is no way I can describe this taste to you. You must try it yourself.

GOLDEN PALACE

BASIC STOCK

4 pounds chicken parts   3 gallons scalding hot water
3 pounds pork

1. Place the chicken and pork in a large kettle or stock pot. Cover with the hot water and bring to a boil.
2. Skim all foam and solids that appear on the surface of the liquid in the pot. When liquid is clear, reduce heat and simmer at least 3 hours.
3. Remove all fat that appears on the top of the liquid.

This recipe, which yields enough for twenty servings, can be used as a base for soups or wherever broth is called for in Cantonese dishes. Refrigerate for no longer than a week or freeze until ready to use.

GOLDEN PALACE

SEAFOOD SOUP WITH BEAN CURD

3¾ cups BASIC STOCK
2 ounces fresh fish fillets, cut into cubes (preferably flounder, sole, or other mild-tasting white fish)
2 ounces fresh crabmeat
3 large shrimp, shelled, deveined, and cut into ½" pieces
½ cup fresh green peas
½ pound fresh mushrooms, sliced ⅓" thick

1 (3") square bean curd, diced into small cubes
1 teaspoon Accent
¾ teaspoon salt
⅓ teaspoon sugar
½ teaspoon white pepper
¼ teaspoon sesame oil
1 teaspoon cornstarch, dissolved in ¼ cup cold water

1. Bring stock to a full boil in a deep pot. Be sure to have all ingredients ready in order to proceed quickly.
2. Add the remaining ingredients except the dissolved cornstarch. Cook over medium heat until the shrimp turn pink.
3. Stir in the dissolved cornstarch, swirling with a large spoon until the soup thickens evenly. Serve at once.

Note: When cooking seafood in a soup, always add a little more salt than sugar.

To vary the flavor and texture, swirl one or two beaten egg whites into the broth after adding the dissolved cornstarch. The egg white will congeal immediately.

If desired, serve the soup with a bowl of freshly fried Chinese noodles. This then becomes a meal in itself.

SEAFOOD COMBINATION IN FRIED TARO NEST

6 *jumbo shrimp, shelled and deveined*	¼ *cup light rice wine*
2 *ounces king crabmeat*	⅓ *cup BASIC STOCK*
10 *scallops*	½ *teaspoon Accent*
2 *tablespoons peanut oil*	⅓ *teaspoon salt*
1½ *ounces snow peas*	¼ *teaspoon sugar*
2 *ounces bamboo shoots, sliced*	*Drop of sesame oil*
3 to 4 *large mushrooms*	*Pinch of white pepper*
5 *(¾") pieces green onion*	1 *teaspoon cornstarch, dissolved in ¼ cup cold water*
5 *slices fresh gingerroot*	*TARO NEST (see next page)*

1. In a small saucepan, bring 1 quart lightly salted water to a full boil. Add the seafood and cook until barely done, about 2 minutes.

2. Remove and pour into a colander to drain.

3. Pour the peanut oil into a very hot wok and heat until almost smoking. Add the vegetables and drained seafoods; stir-fry about 1½ minutes.

4. Add the wine, Basic Stock, and spices. Continue to stir-fry about 30 seconds longer.

5. Add the dissolved cornstarch and stir until thickened. Pour into the warm Taro Nest and serve at once.

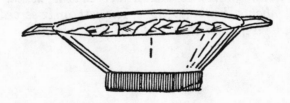

GOLDEN PALACE

TARO NEST

1 or 2 large taro roots   Salt
        Fresh peanut oil

1. Peel the taro root and slice into thin slices. Using a razor-sharp knife or slicing cleaver, finely julienne. The shreds of taro should look like straw potatoes.
2. Pour enough peanut oil into a large, heated wok to deep-fry the taro. Heat to 350°, using a deep-fat thermometer. Dip a skimmer basket or "bird's nest" in the hot oil to prevent the shreds of taro from sticking to it when they deep-fry.
3. Layer the inside of the basket with the julienned taro. If using the skimmer basket, place a metal bowl on top to hold taro in place.
4. Gently lower the basket into the hot oil and deep-fry until the taro turns barely golden. Remove the basket and take off the metal bowl. Use a long-tined fork to loosen the taro nest. Carefully lift from basket and drain on several paper towels.
5. Sprinkle lightly with the salt and keep warm in a low oven, if necessary.

The "bird's nest," a utensil appropriate for deep-frying taro, potato, and noodle nests, consists of two long-handled baskets, one fitted inside the other to mold and hold the frying shreds firmly in place. It comes in three sizes and may be purchased at most stores carrying gourmet kitchen supplies.

This recipe features a basic combination of seafoods, delicate in flavors, and certainly highlighted by the taro nest. The nest can be served on a large platter lined with greens and accented with slices of fruits.

LAMB WITH GINGER AND GREEN ONIONS

10 ounces sliced lamb	½ teaspoon Accent
MARINADE (see next page)	⅓ teaspoon salt
Peanut oil	⅓ teaspoon sugar
15 (¾") slices fresh	¼ teaspoon sesame oil
gingerroot	¼ teaspoon white pepper
15 (¾") pieces green	½ cup rice wine
onions (about 5)	1 teaspoon cornstarch,
1 teaspoon Tabasco sauce	dissolved in ¼ cup
or Szechwan hot sauce	cold water

1. Cut the slices of lamb into strips and toss thoroughly in the Marinade. Marinate 1 to 2 hours.
2. Pour the peanut oil into a heated wok to a depth of 4 inches. Heat until almost smoking. Add the lamb and deep-fry, stirring constantly, until meat is no longer pink, about 3 minutes. Immediately remove wok from heat. Gently empty into a strainer placed over a deep metal bowl. Allow frying oils to drain.
3. Return wok to high heat and add about 1 tablespoon of fresh oil. When almost smoking, add the nearly cooked lamb, ginger, green onions, and the following six seasonings. Stir-fry about 45 seconds. Add the rice wine and cook about 1 minute longer.
4. Stir in the dissolved cornstarch until the sauce thickens. Remove from heat and serve at once.

For best flavor and texture, I prefer slices of lamb from the leg. I also recommend Chef Chow's hot and spicy sauce as the Szechwan hot sauce.

In this recipe, as in all Chinese dishes, it is essential that all ingredients be prepared and within reach before cooking begins.

GOLDEN PALACE

MARINADE

1 teaspoon light soy sauce
1 teaspoon rice wine
1 tablespoon cornstarch
1 clove garlic, finely crushed

¼ teaspoon sugar
½ teaspoon salt
½ teaspoon Accent

Mix all ingredients together until thoroughly combined. Refrigerate until ready to use.

RAINBOW CHICKEN

¾ pound chicken breast,
   skinned and boned
2 eggs, lightly beaten
   MARINADE
½ medium-size onion
½ medium-size green pepper
1 large stalk celery
½ carrot, peeled
2 tablespoons sliced bamboo
   shoots
2 teaspoons sugar

½ teaspoon salt
⅓ teaspoon Accent
4 teaspoons vinegar
2 teaspoons rice wine
¼ teaspoon sesame oil
1½ teaspoons chili paste
   with garlic
1 cup water
   Cornstarch
3 cups plus 2 teaspoons
   peanut oil

1. Wash the chicken breast, pat dry, and lay on cutting surface. Using a razor-sharp knife, slice into 3-inch by 1½-inch strips.
2. In a deep bowl, mix the beaten eggs thoroughly with the Marinade. Add the chicken, coat well, and marinate for 1 hour.
3. Slice the onion, green pepper, celery, and carrot in long strips. Julienne the bamboo shoots. Set aside.
4. Prepare the sauce by combining the next eight ingredients in a small bowl. Set aside along with the dissolved cornstarch.
5. Roll the strips of marinated chicken in cornstarch to coat evenly. Lay on waxed paper. Add 3 cups of the oil to a heated wok and heat until almost smoking. Add the chicken strips, one at a time, so they will crisp well. Stir with a large spatula until meat is nearly done, about 2 minutes.

6. Add the vegetables and deep-fry, stirring constantly, for 2 minutes longer.

7. Remove wok from heat. Gently empty into a strainer placed over a deep metal bowl. Allow frying oil to drain.

8. Return wok to high heat and add the remaining 2 teaspoons oil. When sizzling hot, carefully add the sauce and stir until sauce comes to a boil. Dissolve 1 teaspoon cornstarch in ½ cup cold water and add to sauce, continuing to stir until sauce thickens.

9. Return the drained chicken and vegetables to wok. Stir to coat well with the sauce. Serve at once.

MARINADE

4 teaspoons rice wine	4 teaspoons light soy sauce
1 teaspoon sugar	1 teaspoon Bird's Dessert Mix
1 teaspoon salt	2 tablespoons cornstarch
1 teaspoon Accent	

Mix all ingredients together until thoroughly combined. Refrigerate until ready to use.

Rainbow Chicken is an original recipe of mine, one that is becoming more and more popular. It is an example of the many creative variations one discovers in hot Oriental cuisine. The secret here is the vinegar, which makes the dish pungent without burning the throat and mouth.

SZECHWAN PORK WITH SHALLOTS

10 ounces pork loin, thinly
   sliced and cut into
     squares
   MARINADE
   Peanut oil
10 fresh shallots, peeled
 2 teaspoons brown bean
   sauce
 4 teaspoons hoisin sauce

1 teaspoon Szechwan hot
   sauce (preferably Chef
   Chow's hot and spicy
   sauce)
   Pinch of white pepper
1 teaspoon sesame oil
½ teaspoon sugar
   Scant teaspoon salt
4 slices fresh gingerroot

1. Add the pork to the Marinade, mix well to coat evenly, cover, and marinate for 1 to 2 hours.
2. Heat wok over high heat and add the peanut oil to a depth of 4 inches. When sizzling hot, add the pork and the shallots. Deep-fry about 4 minutes, stirring constantly.
3. Quickly lift wok off heat and empty partially cooked shallots and pork into a strainer set over a deep metal bowl. Drain well.
4. Return wok to high heat and add about 1 tablespoon of fresh oil. Heat until nearly smoking.
5. Add the pork, shallots, and the remaining ingredients. Stir-fry constantly for about 5 minutes. Remove wok. Serve at once.

Note: If using very small shallots, add for the last frying only. Shallots should never be overcooked.

GOLDEN PALACE

MARINADE

2 teaspoons rice wine	½ teaspoon salt
2 teaspoons light soy sauce	½ teaspoon Accent
½ teaspoon sugar	1 tablespoon cornstarch

Mix all ingredients together until thoroughly combined. Refrigerate until ready to use.

This is a very popular dish here at the Golden Palace. The shallots should still have body when served. For a better taste, use more Szechwan hot sauce.

LICHEE DUCK

2 to 3 tablespoons peanut oil	¼ to ½ cup light rice wine
10 ounces roasted BARBECUED DUCK (see next page), boned and cubed	⅓ cup BASIC STOCK
	½ teaspoon garlic paste
	⅓ teaspoon salt
3 ounces (about ¼ cup) sliced bamboo shoots	¼ teaspoon sugar
	½ teaspoon Accent
2 ounces snow peas	¼ teaspoon sesame oil
4 mushrooms, sliced	Pinch of white pepper
4 slices fresh gingerroot	BASIC SWEET AND SOUR SAUCE (see next page)
5 (¾") pieces green onions (about 2)	
1 (16-ounce) can lichee nuts	1 teaspoon cornstarch, dissolved in ¼ cup cold water

1. Add the peanut oil to a heated wok and heat until nearly smoking. Add the duck, vegetables, and lichees. Stir-fry for about 1 minute.
2. Add the wine, Basic Stock, and six seasonings. Stir-fry 3 minutes longer.
3. Mix in Basic Sweet and Sour Sauce thoroughly for 4 or 5 seconds. Add the dissolved cornstarch and stir over high heat until sauce thickens and all ingredients are well coated. Serve at once.

BARBECUED DUCK

½ cup honey	2 teaspoons salt
½ cup vinegar	½ cup cooking wine
1 (4 to 5-pound) duck, cleaned	½ cup sugar
2 tablespoons bean paste	3 green onions
2 tablespoons chopped fresh garlic	

1. Twelve hours before roasting the duck, place a large wok on the stove and fill with 1 gallon water. Add the honey and vinegar and bring to a full boil.
2. Holding the duck by one wing, ladle the hot liquid over the duck, coating well. Continue to ladle for 3 minutes.
3. Tie the legs of the duck together with string and suspend over a container. Let the duck drip dry for 12 hours.
4. Preheat oven to 400°.
5. Combine the bean paste, garlic, salt, wine, and sugar. Place the whole green onions in the duck cavity followed by the bean paste mixture. Sew the opening together and bake in preheated oven for 45 minutes.

Roasted barbecued duck can be purchased in whole or half at many Oriental markets.

In Oriental cuisine, we always serve the sweet and sour dish last, since we believe the strong flavor will jade the taste buds for anything that follows.

BASIC SWEET AND SOUR SAUCE

5 cups BASIC STOCK	⅓ cup brown sugar
1 lemon peel	1 tablespoon sherry
1 orange peel	2 tablespoons tomato paste
1 small onion	2 tablespoons cornstarch
1 cup vinegar	

1. Bring the stock to a boil. Add the lemon peel, orange peel, and onion. Return to a boil and add all the remaining ingredients except the cornstarch. Dissove the cornstarch in ⅓ cup cold water and add to the mixture.
2. Bring to a boil over medium-high heat, stirring constantly 2 to 3 minutes until the sauce thickens.

COCONUT PUDDING WITH FRESH FRUITS

1 ounce agar-agar	2 tablespoons citrus-flavored liqueur (preferably Grand Marnier, Cointreau, or triple sec
1½ cups sugar	
½ cup milk	
4 to 5 ounces canned coconut milk	
1 tablespoon vegetable oil	Assorted fortune and almond cookies
4 cups assorted fruits, fresh and canned	

1. Pour 4 cups cold water into a saucepan. With a sharp pair of kitchen shears, snip the strips of agar-agar to fit into the pan. Place over medium heat and bring to a full boil, stirring from time to time. The agar-agar will dissolve.
2. Add the sugar and mix until it dissolves. Add the milk and coconut milk. Blend well and remove.
3. Oil a 6-cup mold or rinse it out with cold water. Pour in the pudding and refrigerate about 2 hours until set.
4. Cut, peel, and slice fruit into bite-size sections. Cover and refrigerate. Remove 30 minutes before serving. Add the liqueur to the fruit. Mix well and cover.
5. Unmold the pudding into the center of a large platter. Garnish with the fruits. Serve with fortune and almond cookies.

This is a traditional Chinese dessert considered fancy in our cuisine. We do not eat a lot of sweets. You can make this sweeter by adding more coconut milk, but that would not be truly Chinese.

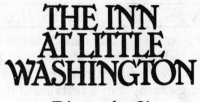

THE INN
AT LITTLE
WASHINGTON

Dinner for Six

Fresh Asparagus in Raspberry Vinaigrette

Sweetbreads with Three Mustard Sauce

Sautéed Fresh Green Beans

White Chocolate Mousse

Beverages:

Château de Sancerre, 1976

With the Mousse—Champagne mixed with 1 tablespoon Tia Maria

Patrick O'Connell and Reinhardt Lynch, Owners

Patrick O'Connell, Executive Chef

THE INN AT LITTLE WASHINGTON

When *Esquire* magazine recently hailed the Inn at Little Washington as one of the 100 best new restaurants in the country, Washington citizens were not surprised. They already knew the Inn to be an outstanding example of a restaurant which is, in all ways, also a work of art.

Owners Patrick O'Connell and Reinhardt Lynch searched for six years to find the perfect spot, having certain requirements in mind for the town as well as the building. They found it in tradition-rich Washington, Virginia, the first city in the United States to be named Washington, its more well-known neighbor being fifty-one years younger. They enlisted the talent of Albert Hinckley, an architect who worked on the Mississippi Queen, to refurbish the interior which is now filled with many antiques, magnificent mirrors and lamps, unusual and luxurious pieces of furniture—all accented by fresh flowers everywhere. They chose Joyce Evans, whose London showroom has accommodated the Queen Mother, to provide the wall coverings.

The owners just as carefully planned and continue to develop their menu. "Our approach to cooking, while paying homage to the lawmakers of classical French cuisine, reflects a belief in the 'cuisine of today,' healthy, eclectic, imaginative, unrestricted by ethnic boundaries, and always growing." Their menu also changes depending upon the seasonal availability of fresh ingredients, but it never varies in its excellence. Each and every item—the puff pastry, the sherbets, the homemade bread—is prepared on the premises which insures the freshness and distinction of every course.

Some of the intimacy of the restaurant is due to its size. The Inn seats only fifty, thus making it necessary to reserve a table two to three weeks in advance. Soon, a reservation could include more than a dining table because Patrick and Reinhardt are planning to open guest rooms for overnight accommodations. It will be the crowning touch to the thoroughly original, pricelessly elegant Inn at Little Washington.

Great Falls, Virginia

FRESH ASPARAGUS IN RASPBERRY VINAIGRETTE

36 large spears asparagus
    VINAIGRETTE DRESSING
    (see next page)

RASPBERRY VINAIGRETTE
    (see second page following)
Cracked black pepper

1. Wash the asparagus well, peel the stems, and remove the white, coarse ends.
2. Pour water to a depth of 2 or 3 inches in a steamer and bring to boil over medium-high heat. Lay the asparagus in the steamer basket, cover tightly, and steam about 4 minutes. Immediately remove the asparagus and plunge into a bowl of ice water. Drain and dry well; place on a large platter.
3. Cover the asparagus with a generous coating of the Vinaigrette Dressing, turning each spear to coat well. Marinate 1 hour.
4. When ready to serve, place six marinated asparagus spears on each of six chilled plates. Drizzle the Raspberry Vinaigrette in a ribbon over the spears on each plate and season with a few grinds of the cracked black pepper.

If you wish, surround the asparagus with a few other julienned vegetables for color and taste contrast, or serve on a bed of Boston lettuce. To convert this into a luncheon dish as we do, simply serve with chicken breasts. Marinate the breasts in olive oil and raspberry vinegar for one to two hours, drain well and grill. Serve the breasts with the asparagus on a bed of fresh spinach and garnish with Raspberry Vinaigrette.

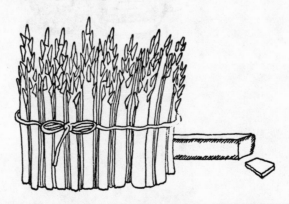

VINAIGRETTE DRESSING

½ cup white wine vinegar	½ cup olive oil
¾ teaspoon salt	1 teaspoon chopped capers
¼ teaspoon ground white pepper	1 teaspoon chopped chives
1 tablespoon Dijon mustard	1 teaspoon finely chopped fresh parsley
1 cup vegetable oil	

1. In a mixing bowl, whisk together the vinegar, salt, and white pepper. Whisk in the mustard.
2. Combine the vegetable oil with the olive oil. Gradually add these to the vinegar/mustard combination, whisking vigorously until the dressing is well blended and thick. Add the capers, chives, and parsley and mix well. Cover and store in the refrigerator.

RASPBERRY VINAIGRETTE

¼ cup whipping cream
¾ pound fresh raspberries
2 tablespoons raspberry
   vinegar

6 tablespoons virgin
   olive oil
Salt and freshly ground
black pepper (optional)

1. Remove the cream from the refrigerator and let stand at room temperature about 10 minutes.
2. Check the raspberries and discard any that are bruised. Purée in a food processor or electric blender. Strain through a fine sieve or chinois to remove all seeds.
3. Whisk the raspberry purée together with the cream in a small bowl. Slowly add the vinegar together with the oil, whisking until the mixture is thick and creamy. Taste for seasoning, adding salt and pepper if desired. Chill until time to serve.

SWEETBREADS WITH THREE MUSTARD SAUCE

3 medium clusters veal
   sweetbreads
2 quarts Chicken Stock
   (see index)
   Salt
   Pepper
½ pound unsalted butter
   (approximately)

1 cup flour (approximately)
2 tablespoons fresh lemon
   juice (approximately)
36 fresh snow peas
   Pinch of sugar
12 fresh mushrooms
   THREE MUSTARD SAUCE

1. A day in advance, place the sweetbreads in a deep bowl and rinse with cold water; drain well.
2. Pour the chicken stock into a deep saucepan and add the sweetbreads. Bring to a gentle simmer and poach about 10 to 15 minutes over medium heat, until the lobes spring back to the touch. Immediately submerge in a bowl of ice water, then rinse well. Place in a colander over a bowl. Set a plate and two or three cans over the lobes to make sure all liquid will drain. Refrigerate overnight.
3. The next day, slice the sweetbreads in thin circles and sprinkle lightly with the salt and pepper.
4. Melt 3 tablespoons of the butter in a large sauté pan. Lightly dust the slices of sweetbread with the flour and sauté on each side until golden brown. Remove to a warm platter, sprinkle lightly with the lemon juice, and keep warm in a low oven.
5. Melt 3 tablespoons of the butter in an 8-inch sauté pan. Add the snow peas and season with sugar, ½ teaspoon salt, and a pinch of pepper. Stirring frequently, sauté about 2 minutes, or until glazed and crisp-tender. Remove the snow peas from the sauté pan, sprinkle with the lemon juice, and keep warm in a low oven.
6. Wipe the mushrooms with a damp cloth and slice thinly. Melt 3 to 4 tablespoons of the butter in the sauté pan. Add the sliced mushrooms and season with ½ teaspoon salt and a pinch of pepper. Sauté about 3 minutes until cooked but still firm. Remove from heat and keep warm in a low oven.
7. Ladle the Three Mustard Sauce over six dinner plates. Alternate layers of the sweetbread slices with the snow peas to form a dome. Top with the mushrooms and serve at once.

Note: Add more butter to the saucepan as needed to sauté the slices of sweetbread. If desired, cook about 3 to 4 tablespoons of butter until brown and pour over the sweetbreads before placing them in the warm oven.

The mushrooms and snow peas contrast well with the taste and texture of the sweetbreads, all complemented beautifully by the Three Mustard Sauce.

THREE MUSTARD SAUCE

¼ cup white wine
½ teaspoon chopped fresh
   shallots
2 tablespoons Dijon mustard
2 teaspoons Pommery whole-
   grain mustard
2 teaspoons green herb
   mustard

1 tablespoon Brown Sauce
   (optional-see index)
2 cups whipping cream
½ cup SAUCE CHORON
   (see next page)

1. Place the wine and chopped shallots in a heavy enameled or copper pot and reduce until the shallots are glazed and only a few bubbles remain.
2. Add the Dijon, Pommery, and green herb mustards and the brown sauce. Add the cream and cook over low heat until reduced by one-third.
3. Keep warm in a bain-marie until time to serve. Before serving, add the Sauce Choron.

Note: The brown sauce is used as a thickener and is optional.

The essential ingredient in the three mustard sauce is the Sauce Choron. While it complicates the preparation, it also counteracts the acidity of the mustard and provides the body and taste everyone loves. Choron, a famous chef who worked in France at the world-renowned Voison, perfected this sauce. Basically, it is a tomato béarnaise and is excellent served with fish or poultry and broiled meats.

THE INN AT LITTLE WASHINGTON

SAUCE CHORON

¼ cup tarragon vinegar
2 tablespoons minced shallots
2 tablespoons plus 1 teaspoon
   minced fresh tarragon
⅛ teaspoon black pepper
3 egg yolks, lightly beaten

1 cup clarified butter, at
   room temperature
Salt and pepper
1 teaspoon minced fresh
   parsley or chervil
¼ cup thick tomato purée

1. In a small, heavy saucepan combine the vinegar, shallots, and the 2 tablespoons tarragon. Reduce the mixture over high heat until about 1 tablespoon remains. Remove from heat and mix in 1 tablespoon cold water. Add the beaten egg yolks and mix briskly with a whisk until thick and creamy.

2. Place over low heat and beat in the butter, about 2 tablespoons at a time. Continue to beat until the sauce is thick. Season with salt and pepper and add the 1 teaspoon tarragon, the parsley or chervil, and tomato purée. Keep warm in a bain-marie.

The recipe yields 1½ cups of sauce.

SAUTÉED FRESH GREEN BEANS

1½ pounds very fresh small
    snap beans
¼ cup plus 1 tablespoon
    unsalted butter
1 rounded teaspoon chopped
    shallots
¼ teaspoon chopped fresh
    garlic

Salt and freshly ground
    black pepper to taste
Tiny pinch of sugar
¼ teaspoon chopped fresh
    tarragon or marjoram
6 thin strips pimiento

1. Trim the ends from the beans and wash thoroughly. Bring a 6-quart pot of salted water to a rolling boil. Drop in the beans and cook exactly 4 minutes.
2. Remove the beans and immediately plunge into a deep bowl of ice water.
3. Fifteen minutes before serving, remove the beans from the ice water; drain well and dry thoroughly.
4. In a small saucepan, melt the ¼ cup butter and brown lightly; do not burn. Remove from heat and reserve.
5. Heat the remaining 1 tablespoon butter in a 10-inch sauté pan, moving the butter around the pan as it melts so that it leaves a thin film over the entire surface. When the butter begins to brown, add the beans and sauté 1½ minutes over very high heat. Constantly toss or lift the beans with a big spoon to prevent burning.
6. Add the shallots and garlic and sauté with the beans about 1 minute, being sure to continue moving the ingredients around in the pan.
7. Add the salt and pepper, sugar, and tarragon or marjoram. Stir briefly, about 15 seconds. Pour over the browned butter, stir once, and remove from heat.
8. Make a neat pile of the beans on each plate, laying them side by side to resemble tiny twigs or logs. Lay a strip of pimiento across each pile so that it resembles a piece of ribbon tying the beans together. Serve at once with the Sweetbreads with Three Mustard Sauce.

Note: The entire cooking time in the sauté pan should not exceed 3 minutes.

The sugar is essential for store-bought beans or beans purchased out of season.

WHITE CHOCOLATE MOUSSE

1¼ cups whipping cream,
   well chilled
¾ pound Swiss white
   chocolate
⅜ cup egg whites
½ cup sugar

2 tablespoons Myers's rum
1½ tablespoons pure vanilla
   extract
CHOCOLATE LEAVES
(optional)

1. With chilled electric beaters and chilled bowl, beat the cream until it forms soft peaks. Refrigerate until ready to use.
2. Melt the chocolate in a low oven or in the top of a double boiler placed over gently simmering water.
3. Beat the egg whites in an electric mixer until stiff. Set aside.
4. Place the sugar and ¼ cup water in a heavy pot. Stir to dissolve over medium heat. Let the syrup cook until it reaches the soft-ball stage or 230°. While beating constantly, slowly add the syrup to the egg whites to create an Italian meringue. Continue beating until the meringue has cooled.
5. Add the melted chocolate and beat until well blended. Add the rum and the vanilla extract and mix, scraping the sides and bottom of the bowl.
6. Gently fold the whipped cream into the chocolate/meringue combination. Using a pastry bag or tube, pipe into 16 to 18-ounce wine goblets. If desired, garnish with the Chocolate Leaves. Refrigerate until time to serve.

Note: The point halfway between ¼ and ½ cup on a liquid measure is ⅜ cup.

To my knowledge, this is the first time our White Chocolate Mousse recipe has been published. The special ingredient in it is a fine imported chocolate called Carma; if you cannot obtain it, select a good brand from a specialty chocolate or candy store. Occasionally, we substitute dark unsweetened chocolate for the white chocolate. For varied effect, we either swirl the dark and white chocolate mousses together in the goblets or fill the centers of the white chocolate with the dark.

CHOCOLATE LEAVES

2 to 3 ounces excellent quality
Swiss dark chocolate

1. Melt the chocolate carefully over warm water. Watch carefully to be sure the chocolate does not burn.
2. When melted, spread the chocolate on waxed or parchment paper and allow to dry about ¾ hour. Do not chill.
3. Using a small paring or serrated knife or decoration cutter, cut the chocolate into leaf shapes. Chill until time to serve.

You may also prepare the Chocolate Leaves by brushing the melted chocolate onto the outer side of leaves, chilling, and then carefully peeling the leaves off. Just be sure you do not use poisonous leaves.

AT WATERGATE

Dinner for Six

*Terrine of Girolle Mushrooms with Maine Lobster
and Watercress Sauce*

Mousseline of Bay Scallops with Asparagus and Puréed Beet Sauce

Roasted Squabs in Chartreuse of Artichoke

Gratin of Raspberries with Ice Cream and Caramel Sauce

Wines:

*With the Terrine and Mousseline—Puligny-Montrachet,
Les Pucelles, 1977*

With the Squabs—Château l'Angelus, St. Émilion, 1966

With the Gratin—Château de Rayne-Vigneau, Sauternes, 1964

Nicolas Salgo, Owner

Jean-Louis Palladin, Executive Chef

Gene Flick, General Manager

JEAN-LOUIS AT WATERGATE

Several years ago, Nicolas Salgo decided to open a posh restaurant in his Watergate complex. In his search to find an outstanding chef, he discovered Jean-Louis Palladin, one of the finest virtuosos in the French world of haute cuisine. Jean-Louis promptly arrived in Washington to become the namesake and executive chef of Salgo's exclusive dining establishment. The restaurant thus opened quietly in 1979.

A shy gentleman outside the kitchen, Jean-Louis nonetheless carries a remarkable record of achievement. The *Guide Michelin* in 1977 awarded him two stars out of a possible three while he was chef at a restaurant in the Gascony city of Condom. Heralded in France as a leading proponent of the nouvelle cuisine, he has since branched out, presently referring to his creative experiments as "contemporary cuisine."

Characteristically, his dishes are a blend of techniques from nouvelle and Japanese cuisines with concepts uniquely his own. A salad or entrée is notedly a visual masterpiece, suggesting that the artist-chef indeed designed each plate with paint brush and palette; for instance, a terrine filled with lobster and mushrooms napped with a green sauce, or a simple salad of asparagus garnished with shad roe and truffles.

Situated in an unobtrusive corner of the Watergate, Jean-Louis frequently caters to Washington syndics and dignitaries. At lunch, it is accessible only to a private club consisting largely of hotel guests, and it seats no more than forty-two. The dining room is small and sumptuous, a fashionable niche where intimacy informs the atmosphere. Crystal and delicate floral displays bedeck the tables. Indirect lighting filters through silk wall hangings suspended from a low ceiling of mirrors, and, at the far end of the room , a French window opens to a terrace and a distant garden. On one side of the carpeted entranceway, a wine room stocks inventory from Nicolas Salgo's private vinyards in Côtes du Rhône and includes rare vintages. From this store, guests may sample such wonders as 1907 Château Mouton Rothschild and 1905 Château Margaux. Near the antique reception desk, a cart laden with fine pastries stands to greet each entering guest.

2650 Virginia Avenue, N.W.

TERRINE OF GIROLLE MUSHROOMS WITH MAINE LOBSTER AND WATERCRESS SAUCE

3 pounds fresh Oregon
   girolle mushrooms
2 tablespoons olive oil
2 teaspoons salt
½ teaspoon white pepper
2 veal hooves
4 carrots, pared
1 turnip, pared
4 stalks celery, washed well
2 leeks, washed well
1 cup white wine
1 onion, quartered
2 shallots, chopped

3 tomatoes, quartered
1 bunch fresh thyme
2 (1½-pound) live lobsters
1 bunch chives, washed
   and chopped
LOBSTER CONSOMMÉ
   (see next page)
LOBSTER CREAM SAUCE
   (see second page following)
1 tablespoon coarse salt
5 bunches watercress,
   washed well

1. Preheat oven to 500°.
2. Wash the mushrooms well and wipe dry. Slice ⅛ inch thick. Heat the olive oil in a large sauté pan and add the sliced mushrooms. Season with the salt and white pepper and sauté 10 minutes.
3. Spoon off the oil and mushroom juice; refrigerate. Continue to sauté the mushrooms until very dry. Taste and add more salt, if desired. Remove from heat and refrigerate.
4. Place the veal bones in a large aluminum or copper pan. Cook in preheated oven 20 minutes, or until golden brown, turning occasionally.
5. Chop the carrots, turnip, celery stalks, and leeks. Place in a deep stockpot with the wine, 1 quart water, onion, shallots, tomatoes, and thyme. Add the browned veal bones and simmer together 30 minutes over moderate heat.
6. Insert the tip of a knife behind the head of each lobster to sever the spinal nerve. Add the lobsters to the stockpot and cook 10 minutes. Remove the lobsters from the stock to cool. Continue to cook the stock until 2 cups remain. Remove from heat.
7. Take out the meat from the lobster tails and claws. Slice the lobster meat into long strips. Set the meat aside and reserve the shells for the Lobster Consommé.

(continued next page)

8. Mix the chilled mushrooms with the chives. Put some of this mixture into a 12-inch by 3-inch by 5-inch ceramic terrine until it is half full. Layer the slices of lobster meat lengthwise down the center of the terrine, then add the remaining mushroom mixture. Pour the warm veal/lobster stock into the terrine and cover with aluminum foil. Place a weight on top of the terrine to level the mushrooms. Refrigerate 24 hours.

9. Prepare the Lobster Consommé and the Lobster Cream Sauce.

10. The next day, make a velouté of watercress by bringing to boil 2 quarts water and the coarse salt. Add the watercress and boil 2 minutes. Immediately remove the watercress and plunge into ice water to arrest further cooking and preserve the color. Squeeze the watercress dry. Purée in an electric blender or food processor, or force through a sieve to achieve the desired extra-fine texture.

11. Warm 1 cup of the Lobster Cream Sauce in a bain-marie. Pour the sauce with the cold oil and juice from the mushrooms into a deep bowl and add the puréed watercress. Blend the sauce with a whisk; its consistency should be thin. Reserve at room temperture or chill, as desired.

12. Before serving, unmold the terrine by bathing the sides with hot running water and inverting over a cookie sheet. Cut the terrine into slices, placing one slice on each of six plates. Pour the watercress velouté over each plate and serve.

LOBSTER CONSOMMÉ

1 carrot, chopped
½ turnip, chopped
2 stalks celery, chopped
1 leek, chopped

2 cups white wine
Lobster shells (from the Terrine of Girolle Mushrooms)

Place all ingredients with 1 quart water into a 4-quart saucepan. Bring to a boil, removing any scum that surfaces. Reduce heat and cook 30 minutes. Force the broth and vegetables through a strainer. Refrigerate.

This recipe will yield enough consommé for both the Terrine of Girolle Mushrooms and the Mousseline of Bay Scallops.

LOBSTER CREAM SAUCE

3 shallots, finely sliced
¼ cup Noilly Pratt vermouth
2 tablespoons fresh tarragon
   leaves

2 cups LOBSTER CONSOMMÉ
2 cups whipping cream
Salt
White pepper

1. In a 3-quart heavy saucepan, combine the shallots, vermouth, and tarragon. Place over medium heat and simmer until reduced by half.
2. Add the Lobster Consommé and reduce again by half. Pour in the cream and reduce 5 minutes until about 2½ cups of sauce remain. Season with the salt and white pepper and strain through a fine sieve. Refrigerate.

This recipe will yield enough sauce for both the Terrine of Girolle Mushrooms and the Mousseline of Bay Scallops.

MOUSSELINE OF BAY SCALLOPS WITH ASPARAGUS
AND PURÉED BEET SAUCE

1 pound bay scallops	2 cups LOBSTER CONSOMMÉ
Salt	
White pepper	1½ cups LOBSTER CREAM SAUCE
2 cups whipping cream	
3 tablespoons coarse salt	1½ pounds fresh green asparagus tips
2 red beets, unpeeled	

1. Remove the tendon from the side of the scallops. Season the scallops well with the salt and white pepper. Purée in a food processor or electric blender.

2. Add the cream. Whip in the processor or blender for 3 minutes and season with a little more salt and white pepper. Pour this mousseline mixture into six custard cups, cover with plastic wrap, and refrigerate.

3. Place cold water and coarse salt in a small pot and bring to a full boil. Add the beets, cover, and cook about 35 to 45 minutes until well done. Cool slightly, peel, then purée in a food processor or electric blender. Set aside.

4. Prepare the Lobster Consommé.

5. Preheat oven to 275°. Prepare the Lobster Cream Sauce.

6. Take the custard cups from the refrigerator and place in a deep baking pan. Do not remove the plastic wraps. Fill the pan with warm water to half the height of the cups. Bake in preheated oven for 30 minutes.

7. Meanwhile, boil 2 quarts salted water in a 3-quart saucepan. Add the asparagus tips, boil 3 minutes, then immediately plunge into ice water to arrest further cooking. Drain and set aside.

8. Remove the baked mousselines from the oven and take off the plastic wraps. To unmold, gently insert a table knife down the side of each cup. Slide the knife around to loosen and invert over cheesecloth to drain. Carefully arrange the mousselines on a serving plate.

9. Heat 1½ cups of the Lobster Cream Sauce in a bain-marie. Add 2 tablespoons of the beet purée and mix. Reheat the asparagus tips in 2 cups of the Lobster Consommé. Drain well. Ladle the hot sauce over the mousselines and garnish with the asparagus tips. Serve at once.

It is important to select fresh young asparagus and tender young beets.

ROASTED SQUABS IN CHARTREUSE OF ARTICHOKE

3 *fresh squabs*	9 *artichokes*
2 *large onions*	*Oil*
2 *carrots*	¼ *pound prosciutto, diced*
1 *leek, well washed*	2 *tablespoons butter*
1 *turnip*	2 *bunches fresh thyme*
3 *tomatoes*	3 *cloves garlic, chopped*
2 *tablespoons salt*	1 *teaspoon white pepper*

1. Thoroughly clean the squabs, saving the livers and hearts. Cut off the legs and cut out the breasts. Remove the breast bones but do not remove the bones from the legs. Slice the breasts in half. Set aside.
2. Place the carcasses and breast bones in a 4-quart saucepan. Add 1 of the onions, the carrots, leek, turnip, tomatoes, and 1½ tablespoons of the salt. Add enough cold water to cover and bring to a boil over high heat. Remove any scum that surfaces, lower heat, and simmer 1 hour, stirring occasionally. Strain this bouillon into a clean pot through a fine sieve lined with cheesecloth. Set aside.
3. Trim the leaves from the artichokes and remove the chokes, leaving only the hearts. Using a mandoline, julienne the hearts and set aside.
4. Dice the remaining onion. In a small sauté pan, heat a drop of the oil and add the diced onion and diced prosciutto. Sauté over low heat for 15 minutes. Add the julienned artichoke hearts and enough of the bouillon to cover. Simmer 15 minutes.
5. Melt the butter in a large sauté pan over medium-high heat. On each side, sauté the breast halves for 2 minutes and the legs for 3 minutes. Add the thyme and garlic and season with the remaining ½ tablespoon salt and the white pepper. Add the hearts and livers, sauté for 1 minute, and remove. Slice and set aside.

(continued next page)

6. To create the chartreuses, carefully lift the julienned artichoke from the bouillon with a slotted spoon, drain well, and mound in the centers of six plates. Over each mound, place a breast half and a leg. Over these, place slices of heart and liver. Spoon a little artichoke/prosciutto bouillon over the completed chartreuses and serve at once.

Squabs, or tender young pigeons, are easily accessible in France and are available in the United States at delicatessens and butcher shops.

There is nothing like fresh produce and meat. I try hard to offer only dishes that use the freshest ingredients, often changing the menu if these ingredients can not be procured.

GRATIN OF RASPBERRIES WITH ICE CREAM
AND CARAMEL SAUCE

1⅓ cups sugar
1 quart whipping cream

3 pints fresh unblemished
raspberries

1. Place the sugar and 3 tablespoons water into a light saucepan. Stirring constantly, cook over low heat until the water evaporates and the sugar turns a rich caramel color. The sugar should acquire both the look and smell of caramel. Watch carefully to avoid burning, and remove from heat as soon as it is done.
2. Pour 2 cups of the cream into a deep bowl and add the caramel. Let the bowl stand until the caramel and cream have gradually blended. When blended, freeze the caramel cream for 15 minutes.
3. Whip the remaining 2 cups cream in a chilled bowl. Add to the cold caramel cream and gently combine. Measure ⅓ cup plus 2 teaspoons into a small cup and set aside. Use the remaining caramel cream mixture to make ice cream by churning 10 to 15 minutes in an ice cream machine and then freezing for 1 to 2 hours.
4. Preheat broiler.
5. Wash the raspberries well and dry completely. Arrange in a double or triple row around the rims of six broiler-proof plates.
6. Drip the reserved caramel cream mixture over the raspberries and place under the broiler until the caramel is golden. Remove from oven. Chill the centers of the plates by spraying from underneath with a CO_2 aerosol. Place scoops of the caramel ice cream on the chilled centers. Serve at once, being sure to use potholders while handling the plates.

This is actually a simple dish. The trick is in the broiling and in the use of the aerosol, a technique that wasn't even thought of until recently. If you expect to be pressed for time, make the ice cream a day or so before serving.

THE JOCKEY CLUB

Dinner for Six

Soupe de Moule au Safran

Baked Crab Jockey

Côte de Veau Poele aux Morilles

Deux Purée

Jockey Club Salad

Apple Soufflé

Wines:
With the Soup and Crab—Riesling, Hugel, 1975
With the Veal—Chanté Alouette, Hermitage Blanc, Chapoutier, 1979
With the Apples Soufflés—Château d'Yquem, Sauternes, 1971

John B. Coleman, Owner
Paul De Lisle, Food and Beverage Director
John Gonzales, Chef
Martin Garbisu, Maître d'

JOCKEY CLUB

The John Fitzgerald Kennedys started a trend in the early 1960's. They visited and applauded the newly re-opened Jockey Club restaurant; politicians, visiting diplomats, and well-known personalities from all professions soon followed suit. The trend has not diminished to this day. The Jockey Club remains a traditional favorite for those, whether famous or not, who demand the unusual and exceptional in dining.

General Manager Paul Seligson proudly describes their cuisine as "cuisine of the bourgeoisie—good, robust, country food." He calls it "simple cooking," but it is simple only in the sense that it delights palates of all levels of sophistication. For although "simple," the meals there are prepared with as much care as are more esoteric courses. The Jockey Club takes advantage of local seafoods in preparing their fish dishes; the Baked Crab Jockey, a house specialty the recipe for which is included here, exemplifies the excellence of such regional flavor. The liver and kidney dishes have also received much praise, although never to the exclusion of any of their outstanding offerings.

The furnishings create an atmosphere of conviviality. The restaurant looks like an English tavern with its low, heavy wooden beams, the paintings of the hunt enlivening the walls, and the presence of pewter steins. The appeal of this ambiance as well as the unusual cuisine insures that, for individuals from all walks of life, the Jockey Club will remain a watering hole for a long time to come.

2100 Massachusetts Avenue, N.W.

SOUPE DE MOULE AU SAFRAN
Mussel Soup with Saffron

2 *pounds fresh mussels*
3 *medium-size shallots*
1 *small bunch parsley*
1 *cup white wine*
¾ *cup unsalted butter*
  Freshly ground white
  pepper

1½ *cups plus 1 tablespoon*
  all-purpose flour
1 *teaspoon finely chopped*
  saffron
2 *quarts whipping cream*
  Salt

1. Scrub the mussels thoroughly under running water, removing the beards, and set aside.
2. Finely mince the shallots, then the parsley. Squeeze the parsley vigorously in a clean linen towel to remove liquid. Set aside.
3. In a deep saucepan with a tight-fitting lid, place the shallots, wine, and 6 tablespoons of the butter. Season with the pepper. Bring to a full boil over high heat. Add the mussels, cover, and steam about 8 minutes, shaking every 2 minutes to ensure even cooking. When mussels have opened, remove pan from heat. Lift the mussels from the hot stock with a large strainer or slotted spoon. Discard any that have not opened. Remove mussels from their shells and cover with either a damp linen towel or some of the stock to prevent drying out. Reserve the stock.
4. In a small pan, make a roux by melting the remaining butter and adding the flour. Cook over low heat for 5 minutes, stirring constantly. Remove from heat and reserve.
5. Cook the reserved mussel stock until at least ⅔ cup remains. The stock should taste fairly strong. Add the roux to the simmering stock and blend vigorously. Add the chopped saffron and the cream and cook gently for 40 minutes over low heat. Do not allow to cook rapidly. The mixture should not become dark.
6. Season with salt and pepper and strain through a fine sieve into a clean pot. Add the mussels. Reheat and serve piping hot. Garnish with the chopped parsley.

Though not for the faint of heart, this dish is an elegant way to begin a meal.

BAKED CRAB JOCKEY

1 pound fresh lump crabmeat, cleaned	Salt and pepper
2 tablespoons unsalted butter	1¼ cups WHITE FISH VELOUTÉ
2 shallots, finely chopped	½ cup whipping cream
1 teaspoon curry powder	¼ cup HOLLANDAISE SAUCE (see second page following)

1. Preheat oven to 350°.

2. Check the crabmeat to be sure it is free of shell fragments. Melt the butter in an 8-inch sauté pan. Add the shallots and simmer about 2 minutes. Add the curry powder and cook approximately 2 minutes to dissolve. Add the crabmeat and a dash of salt and pepper. Toss once and add the White Fish Velouté. Toss once more, being careful not to break the lumps of crabmeat. Bring to a full boil and remove from heat.

3. Whip the cream and set aside. Stir the Hollandaise Sauce into the pan mixture, then gently fold in the whipped cream. Spoon into lightly buttered shells or ramekins and glaze in preheated oven 3 or 4 minutes before serving. Serve at once on small plates lined with doilies.

Whether or not it appears on the menu, Baked Crab Jockey is a house specialty we will prepare for you at your request. At home, I vary the recipe sometimes by adding small fresh shrimp to the crabmeat.

WHITE FISH VELOUTÉ

1 cup FISH FUMET	4 tablespoons flour
3 tablespoons butter	1 pint whipping cream

1. In a 3-quart saucepan, bring the Fish Fumet to a boil, then cook until reduced by half.
2. In a small sauté pan, make a roux by melting the butter and adding the flour. Cook over low heat for 5 minutes, stirring constantly. Remove from heat and reserve.
3. Add the roux and the cream to the reduced fumet. Simmer 20 minutes. Strain through a fine sieve into a clean saucepan and keep warm.

FISH FUMET

2 pounds raw white fish bones and trimmings, chopped	1 cup white wine
	1 sprig thyme
	1 bay leaf
1 onion, chopped	Salt and pepper to taste
½ lemon	

1. Place all ingredients in a large stockpot. Add enough cold water to cover. Simmer over medium heat for 30 minutes.
2. Strain through a fine sieve into a clean container. Refrigerate or freeze for future use.

HOLLANDAISE SAUCE

¾ cup unsalted butter
¾ teaspoon lemon juice
2 egg yolks, at room
temperature

Salt
Pinch of white pepper

1. Place the butter in a small saucepan and melt over low heat. Skim the foam that gathers on the surface. Remove from heat and let stand a few moments while the milk solids settle to the bottom. Carefully pour the clarified butter into a clean container, allowing the milky sediment to remain at the bottom of the pan.

2. In the top of a double boiler, place the lemon juice, 1½ teaspoons water, and the egg yolks. Whisk constantly over simmering water until the mixture thickens enough to hold light peaks. Remove and keep warm.

3. Gradually beat in small quantities of the clarified butter until the sauce thickens toward the consistency of heavy cream. Continue to add the butter, beating more vigorously. When all the butter is incorporated, the sauce should be thick and firm. Season with salt and white pepper.

CÔTE DE VEAU POELE AUX MORILLES
Veal Chops with Morels in Brandy Sauce

1½ ounces dried morels
5 tablespoons butter
6 center-cut veal chops
Salt
Freshly ground white
pepper
Flour
6 tablespoons brandy

6 tablespoons Madeira
6 tablespoons white wine
2 whole shallots
1 cup Chicken Stock
(see index)
1 quart unpasteurized
heavy cream
Chopped fresh parsley

1. Remove the stems from the dried morels. Place in a small bowl and cover with cold water. Soak 8 hours or overnight. Change the water at least four times, twice in the first hour or two and twice near the last, or until it remains clear. Drain the morels and pat dry. Reserve.

2. Preheat oven to 300°.

3. Clarify 3 tablespoons of the butter. Heat the clarified butter in a large ovenproof sauté pan. Season the veal chops lightly with the salt and white pepper, dust lightly with the flour, and sauté. When golden on one side, turn over and place the sauté pan in the preheated oven. Cook 30 minutes longer, turning from time to time so chops color evenly. Remove chops from pan and place on a warm platter; keep warm in oven.

4. Spoon off the fat in the sauté pan. Place over moderate heat and deglaze with the brandy, Madeira, and wine, scraping and stirring the solidified pan juices. Simmer until reduced by one-third.

5. Melt 2 tablespoons of the butter in the sauté pan. Add the shallots and the morels. Sauté until tender and no liquid remains.

6. Add the chicken stock and reduce by two-thirds. Add the cream and reduce by one-half, or until the sauce coats the back of a wooden spoon. Add the morels and shallots and cook 3 to 4 minutes longer.

7. Place the sautéed veal chops on a warm serving platter and douse with the hot brandy sauce. Garnish with the chopped parsley and serve at once.

Note: Frequently, the terms whipping, light, and heavy cream cause confusion. Whipping cream contains between 32% and 40% butterfat. When it contains 32%, it is referred to as light cream; when it contains 40%, as heavy cream. Supermarkets customarily carry only whipping cream with no further distinction as to whether it is light or heavy. In this recipe, however, there is no substitute for the unpasteurized (raw) heavy cream. The undaunted epicure must obtain this cream directly from a dairy or specialty food store.

DEUX PURÉE

1 *pound fresh broccoli,*
  washed and coarsely
  chopped
1 *pound fresh carrots,*
  peeled and chopped

½ *cup unsalted butter*
1 *quart whipping cream*
  Salt
  White pepper

1. Cook the broccoli and the carrots separately in boiling salted water until tender but not mushy.
2. Strain and purée separately in an electric blender or food processor.
3. Pour the puréed broccoli into one saucepan, the puréed carrots into another. To each, add ¼ cup of the butter and 1 pint of the cream. Bring the puréed vegetables to a boil and simmer until a tight consistency is obtained. Remove. Season with salt and white pepper and serve at once.

These purées contrast marvelously with the veal chops and accompany lamb and chicken just as nicely. They may seem heavy, but the cream is elusive and thus not filling.

JOCKEY CLUB

JOCKEY CLUB SALAD

1 *large head Boston lettuce*	1 *pound fresh mushrooms,*
1 *bunch watercress*	*stems removed*
2 *Belgian endives*	*HOUSE DRESSING*

1. Wash the greens thoroughly and dry well. Cover and refrigerate until very cold and crisp.
2. Peel and slice the mushrooms. Combine the greens and the sliced mushrooms in a large salad bowl. Add the House Dressing, toss well, and divide among six chilled salad plates. Serve immediately.

HOUSE DRESSING

2 *large egg yolks, beaten*	2 *cups olive oil*
1 *tablespoon Dijon mustard*	*Freshly ground white*
½ *cup red wine vinegar*	*pepper*
Salt	

In a deep mixing bowl, combine the beaten egg yolks with the mustard and the vinegar. Add about ½ teaspoon salt and whisk togther vigorously. Beat in the oil slowly until the dressing becomes thick and creamy. Taste for seasoning and add more salt, if desired. Add the pepper to taste. Store in a large covered jar in the refrigerator.

APPLE SOUFFLÉ

6 *large apples*
1 *cup sugar (approximately)*
2 *cups milk*
4 *egg yolks*
1 *cup plus 1 tablespoon*
   all-purpose flour

2 *egg whites, at room*
   temperature
   APPLE APPAREIL
½ *cup Calvados*

1. Slice the bottoms off the apples so they will stand upright. Cut a large hole in the top of each and remove most of the flesh, leaving a ¼-inch-thick wall. Be sure to leave the skin intact; do not tear. Sprinkle the inside of each apple with sugar and set in a baking pan.

2. Place 1½ cups of the milk in a saucepan and bring to a boil over moderate heat. Remove from heat.

3. In a medium-size bowl, beat the egg yolks, flour, and ½ cup plus 1 tablespoon of the sugar. Mix in the ½ cup remaining cold milk, then a little of the hot milk. Add the remaining hot milk. Combine thoroughly.

4. Pour this pastry cream mixture into the saucepan and bring to a full boil, whisking constantly to prevent lumps from forming. Remove from heat and continue to whisk until smooth and thick. Cool.

5. Preheat oven to 375°.

6. Beat the egg whites to soft peaks in a small bowl, gradually adding 1 tablespoon of the sugar.

7. In a stainless steel bowl, combine the pastry cream thoroughly with the Apple Appareil. Mix one-fourth of the beaten egg white into the apple/cream base. Carefully fold in the remaining egg white. The soufflé mixture should look like a génoise batter.

8. Fill each prepared apple with the soufflé mixture to within ⅛ inch of the top. Bake in preheated oven 10 to 12 minutes.

9. Place the apple soufflés on individual plates. Before serving, heat the Calvados in a saucepan and pour over the apples. Flame at the table.

If desired, prepare the apples and pastry cream in advance. Sprinkle the hollowed apples with lemon juice to prevent discoloration. Cover the pastry cream and refrigerate both until ready to use.

Be sure to purchase the largest apples you can find to be filled. I always pay a little extra for these, but they repay me when I present this dish. It makes a fabulous presentation.

APPLE APPAREIL

4 or 5 apples, peeled, cored,
       and coarsely chopped
½ to ¾ cup sugar
  ¼ cup Calvados

1 tablespoon dark rum
  Pinch of cinnamon
  Pinch of nutmeg (optional)

Combine all ingredients in a heavy saucepan and cook until the apples are tender. Remove pan from heat and purée until smooth. Cool and refrigerate.

Note: The amount of sugar will depend upon the sweetness of the apples. Be sure not to make the appareil too sweet, since there is sugar in other parts of this dessert.

Dinner for Six

Pâté de Lapin, Madeira-Truffle Sauce

Assiette de Crustaces au Basilic

Aiguillette de Canard aux Figues

Riz Sauvage

Salade

Soufflé au L'Orange

Wines:
Apéritif—Champagne with Fresh Raspberries
With the Pâté—a vintage Port or Madeira
With the Shellfish—Meursault-Perrières, Perrin-Ponsot, 1978
With the Duck—Pommard, Leroy, "Tastevinage", 1971
With the Soufflé—Château Suduirat, Sauternes, 1965

Jean-Pierre and Colette Goyenvalle, Owners
Jean-Pierre, Executive Chef

LE LION D'OR

At Le Lion d'Or, a guest is attended to as regally as if he were French royalty dining at a country estate of some earlier century. Elegance is the keynote here, and no expense is spared in delivering that with gracious style and aplomb.

Co-owner and Executive Chef Jean-Pierre Goyenvalle is a man who admits he favors that quality himself. Together with his wife Colette, he has established a restaurant that is "a reflection of the two of us," a reflection of what they enjoy most when they dine out. The service they have instituted is fully typified in Maître d' Paul Hardy who has worked with Jean-Pierre for over seventeen years. Paul is courteous while somewhat diffident, as when he recites the daily specials, and he instructs his staff to adopt the same manner of cultivated politeness. At Le Lion d'Or, no waiter will ever intrude upon a guest's privacy, but one always appears instantly when a patron desires some little service.

Jean-Pierre and his staff specialize in haute cuisine that is so consistently imaginative, one wonders how the level of excellence is maintained. Jean-Pierre answers that they "work hard, and never stop learning. Never!" He uses local products as often as possible but does not hesitate to have special items flown in from anywhere in the world if the finest quality is not available nearby. Although he is proud of all their creations, he does concede that the dessert soufflés have appropriately earned laudatory kudos.

The furnishings at Le Lion d'Or are as refined as the service and the cuisine. From the heavily carved wooden-bar doorknobs on the entrance door to the gigantic grandfather clock in the flower-filled foyer, the surroundings complement the refined quintessence of this exquisite and ultra-elegant dining establishment.

1150 Connecticut Avenue, N.W.

PÂTÉ DE LAPIN, MADEIRA-TRUFFLE SAUCE

1 *pound fresh rabbit*	*Butter*
½ *cup good-quality dry white wine*	1 *egg, beaten with 1 drop water*
2 *teaspoons chopped fresh shallots*	*MADEIRA-TRUFFLE SAUCE (see second page following)*
½ *pound ground pork*	
Salt and pepper to taste	
PÂTÉ FEUILLETÉE (see next page)	

1. Cut the rabbit into strips approximately ½ inch by ½ inch. Set aside.
2. In a small sauté pan, combine the wine and shallots and simmer until the liquid is greatly reduced and only a few bubbles remain. Let cool.
3. Place the pork, rabbit, and wine/shallot mixture in a deep bowl and blend well, seasoning with the salt and pepper.
4. Preheat oven to 400°. Roll out the Pâte Feuilletée to about 9 inches by 12 inches on a generously floured board. Form the rabbit/pork mixture into a small loaf about 7 inches long, and center on the dough. Lift the sides of the dough up and around the rabbit loaf, being sure to seal all the edges and openings carefully.
5. Turn over so the smooth bottom becomes the top, and the pâté is resting on the seam. Decorate with leaves and twigs made from any remaining dough, if desired.
6. Place on a lightly greased baking pan and brush surface of the pâté dough with the beaten egg.
7. Bake in preheated oven for 40 minutes. Slice and serve hot with Madeira-Truffle Sauce on the side.

LE LION D'OR

PÂTE FEUILLETÉE

2 cups all-purpose
  flour
¾ teaspoon salt
½ pound unsalted butter,
  softened

½ cup ice water
  (approximately)

1. Using a pastry blender, combine the flour and salt in a bowl with 4 tablespoons of the butter. Slowly add the water, a tablespoon at a time, mixing until a coarse dough has formed.
2. Pile the dough on a large sheet of aluminum foil and pound into a rough square. Place the remaining butter in the center of the square of dough. Be sure dough and butter are the same consistency. Fold the dough around the butter so that the butter is completely encased.
3. Place dough on lightly floured surface. Beat gently but firmly to spread butter quickly to ends of dough. Roll out to a 12-inch by 6-inch rectangle.
4. Fold one-third of the dough over the center third. Fold the remaining third over the other two to form three layers.
5. Turn dough so that the top flap is to the right. Roll out again to a 12-inch by 6-inch rectangle.
6. Repeat steps 4 and 5.
7. Wrap dough in waxed paper and put in plastic bag. Refrigerate for 15 minutes.
8. Repeat steps 4 through 7 twice more, so that you will have completed six turns, two at a time, allowing 15 minutes of rest for the dough between each two turns. Wrap and refrigerate until ready to bake.

MADEIRA-TRUFFLE SAUCE

4 teaspoons butter
2 teaspoons chopped truffles
4 teaspoons Madeira
    (preferably Rainwater)

½ cup Beef Stock (see
    index)

In a small saucepan, melt 2 teaspoons of the butter. Add the truffles and Madeira. Cook until the sauce is reduced to half its volume. Add the beef stock and cook for an additional 10 minutes. Before serving, season with the remaining butter.

Note: Sauce can be prepared two hours in advance and kept warm in a bain-marie. Be sure to add the remaining butter only just before serving.

This is a relatively simple recipe that takes some time to construct. The meat and dough are not baked in a pâté mold but allowed to brown standing free-form.

ASSIETTE DE CRUSTACES AU BASILIC

3 (1-pound) fresh live
   lobsters
2 teaspoons olive oil
2 carrots, peeled and diced
1 stalk celery, washed and
   chopped
1 onion, peeled and chopped
1 cup white wine
1 sprig parsley
1 bay leaf
1 teaspoon thyme
3 peppercorns
½ cup whipping cream

2 egg yolks
   Salt and pepper
2 fresh tomatoes, peeled,
   seeded, chopped, and
   drained
1 teaspoon fresh basil,
   chopped
12 large fresh shrimp, washed
   shelled, and deveined
24 fresh, small bay scallops
1 pound jumbo fresh lump
   crabmeat (approximately)

1. Using a strong, razor-sharp knife, sever the heads from each live lobster. Set the remaining lobster parts aside.
2. Cut the heads into small sections and place in a stockpot with the olive oil. Sauté a few minutes over medium heat. Add the carrots, celery, and onion and sauté until the lobster pieces turn bright red.
3. Pour in the wine and add the parsley, bay leaf, thyme, and peppercorns. Fill the pot with enough water to cover all the ingredients. Do not add salt. Simmer 20 minutes.
4. Line a strainer with cheesecloth and place over a clean saucepan. Strain the lobster stock into the pan. Cook the stock until 1 cup of liquid remains. Set aside.
5. Whisk the egg yolks and whipping cream together vigorously. Lightly season with the salt and pepper. Pour and whisk a little of the hot stock into the cream/egg mixture. Gradually whisk this mixture into the stock in the pot.
6. Cook over medium heat, stirring constantly, until the sauce thickens. Do not boil. Add the tomatoes and basil. Mix and cook slowly 3 minutes longer.
7. Meanwhile, separate the tail and the claws from the lobster bodies.

8. Bring a large pot of salted water to boil. Reduce to a gentle simmer. Add the reserved uncooked lobster and simmer 4 to 5 minutes. Add the shrimp and simmer 3 minutes. Add the bay scallops and simmer 1 minute. Add the lump crabmeat and simmer 30 seconds. Remove all and drain well. Carefully crack the lobster claws and tail and remove the meat. Slice each tail in half.

9. Divide the hot basil sauce among six warmed salad plates. Put equal portions of the lobster meat, shrimp, bay scallops, and lump crabmeat on each plate. Serve immediately, before the sauce has a chance to curdle.

The lumps of crabmeat should just be warmed, since they are already cooked—thus, do not submerge in water for more than 30 seconds. This dish is best made in the summer when the tomatoes are at their best, and, of course, basil is not too difficult to find.

AIGUILLETTE DE CANARD AUX FIGUES

3 (5-pound) ducks, washed
   and dried
2 carrots, peeled
1 large onion
1 stalk celery, washed
1 bay leaf
½ teaspoon thyme
1 cup good-quality dry
   white wine

18 fresh figs
½ cup ruby port
4 teaspoons unsalted butter
Salt
Black pepper
DUCK MOUSSE
White pepper

1. Preheat oven to 400°.
2. Bone the ducks, leaving the breasts whole and breastbones intact. Trim visible fat from breasts without tearing the skin. Cover and refrigerate. Remove the flesh from the duck leg meat, discarding skin and sinews. Cover and refrigerate for future use.
3. Chop the vegetables and place with the remaining duck bones in a large roasting pan. Brown well in preheated oven.
4. Empty into a deep stockpot. Add the seasonings and wine, cover with cold water, and cook 1½ hours.
5. Strain stock into a saucepan through a sieve lined with cheesecloth. Simmer until 1 cup broth remains. Refrigerate until ready to use.
6. In a heavy saucepan, cook the figs, port, and butter for 5 minutes. Remove pan from heat. Remove the figs; cover loosely with foil to keep warm. Reserve the fig liquid.
7. In a small saucepan, combine the duck stock and the fig liquid. Cook until 1 cup sauce remains. Keep warm in a bain-marie.
8. Preheat oven to 500°. Season the duck breasts with the salt and black pepper. Place in a sturdy baking pan over medium heat. Brown well, turning carefully with two wooden spoons so skin does not tear.
9. Roast in preheated oven 30 minutes, turning once. Remove. Meat should be pink. Separate breast halves, discarding breastbones. Carve into diagonal slices.

10. Place a slice of warm Duck Mousse on each of six warmed plates. Top with the slices of breast and surround each plate with 3 figs. Season the warm fig sauce with the salt and white pepper. Pour over each dish and serve at once.

Serve this dish with Riz Sauvage.

Fresh figs will keep about one week in the refrigerator. Use any variety.

DUCK MOUSSE

Reserved duck leg meat, refrigerated
10 ounces foie gras

½ cup whipping cream
Sprinkle of salt and pepper

1. Preheat oven to 400°.
2. Remove the duck leg meat from the refrigerator. Place meat with the foie gras in a food processor. Process to paste.
3. Add the cream, salt, and pepper. Mix 10 seconds longer. Pour into a 1½ to 2-quart mold.
4. Place mold in a deep baking pan. Fill the pan with hot water to two-thirds the height of the mold. Bake in preheated oven 10 minutes. Remove and cool slightly before slicing into six slices.

Note: If desired, prepare steps 2 and 3 in advance and refrigerate. Bake just prior to roasting the duck breasts. The mousse should be hot when served.

Foie gras is specially fattened goose liver available at fine gourmet stores. Do not confuse with pâté de foie gras, which is made with such fattened liver.

RIZ SAUVAGE

¾ cup wild rice
½ teaspoon salt
2 small zucchini, washed

4 teaspoons unsalted butter
Salt and pepper

1. Rinse the rice under cold water and drain well.
2. Place in a saucepan and cover with 1⅔ cups cold water and the salt. Cover the saucepan and bring to a boil. Remove the cover, lower heat, and cook, stirring occasionally, for about 30 minutes or until tender. Drain and reserve.
3. Cut each zucchini in four sections and dice into ¾-inch chunks. Melt the butter in an 8-inch skillet and add the zucchini. Sauté until tender.
4. Add the rice and sauté 2 minutes longer. Season lightly with the salt and pepper before serving.

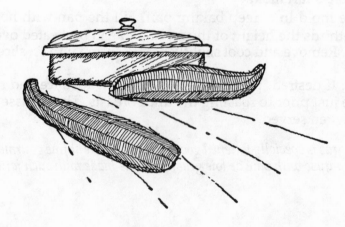

LE LION D'OR

SALADE

2 pounds lamb's lettuce
4 heads Belgian endive
2 teaspoons sherry vinegar
¼ teaspoon salt

3 to 4 grinds fresh black pepper
2 teaspoons olive oil
2 teaspoons pine nuts

1. Separate the leaves of the lettuce and endive; wash well and drain. Place in a deep wooden bowl.
2. Combine the vinegar, salt, and pepper in a small bowl. Whisk until the salt dissolves. Add the oil slowly while whisking vigorously until the dressing thickens.
3. Divide the salad among six chilled salad plates. Pour the dressing over the greens.
4. Sprinkle with the pine nuts and serve at once.

Lamb's lettuce, also called "corn salad," is known as mâche *in France. It is in season in the spring. Be sure to use it, since it has a nutty flavor that makes any simple salad a joy. Be sure, also, to use the best olive oil you can find.*

SOUFFLÉ AU L'ORANGE

PASTRY CREAM
4 *egg yolks*
6 *egg whites, at room temperature*
2 *tablespoons sugar*
¼ *cup plus 4 teaspoons Cointreau*
2 *teaspoons candied orange rind, chopped*

1 *cup fresh orange sections*
Confectioners' sugar
Julienned candied orange rind for garnish
APRICOT SAUCE

1. Preheat oven to 375°. Mix the warm Pastry Cream in a bowl with the egg yolks to form a cream custard.
2. In a large bowl, beat the egg whites until stiff. Add the sugar gradually, beating until glossy. Reserve.
3. Add 4 teaspoons Cointreau and orange rind to the custard. Add one-fourth of the beaten egg white and mix well. Gently fold the remaining egg white into the custard until completely incorporated.
4. Butter two 6-inch soufflé dishes and sprinkle each generously with sugar. Pour one-eighth of the soufflé mixture into the bottom of one soufflé dish. Pour another eighth into the second. Top the mixture in the dishes with ½ cup of the orange sections.
5. Fill the dishes with the remaining mixture. Smooth the tops of the soufflés with a large spatula and bake 30 to 35 minutes.
6. Remove from oven at once. The soufflés should be a light golden brown. Sprinkle with the confectioners' sugar and decorate with the remaining ½ cup orange sections and the julienned candied orange rind.
7. Warm the ¼ cup Cointreau in a saucepan. Ignite and pour over the soufflés. Serve immediately with Apricot Sauce.

Note: The pastry cream must be warm. If you have prepared the cream in advance, just place in the top of a double boiler and reheat slowly over gently simmering water.

PASTRY CREAM

2 cups milk	½ cup sugar
3 eggs	¾ cup flour
1 egg yolk	

1. In a small saucepan, bring the milk to a boil.
2. In a large mixing bowl, thoroughly blend the eggs, egg yolk, and sugar. Add the flour and blend until very smooth.
3. Pour the boiling milk slowly into the egg mixture, stirring constantly to blend well. Pour the egg/milk mixture into a clean saucepan and return to medium heat. Whisking constantly, bring to a full boil and boil 2 minutes.
4. Remove from heat and keep warm, or refrigerate for later use.

APRICOT SAUCE

1 cup whipping cream	2 teaspoons apricot liqueur
½ cup apricot preserves	

1. Whip cream until stiff.
2. Melt the apricot preserves in a tiny saucepan. Strain the liquid from the preserves into a small bowl.
3. Gently fold this apricot glaze into the whipped cream and flavor with the apricot liqueur. Serve a heaping tablespoon on the side of each serving of the soufflé.

I always measure my soufflé dishes by diameter. Two 6-inch soufflés serve six people handsomely. It will not be necessary to build a "collar" around the dishes. Also, the amount of liqueur and glaze that you use in the apricot sauce is a matter of personal taste. Remember, however, that the sauce should complement, never dominate the soufflé.

Maison Blanche

Dinner for Six

Terrine de Légumes

Lobster Consommé with Fresh Truffles

Paupiettes de Saumon aux Senteurs de Provence

Salade de Mâche et Rouge de Trevisse

Nougat Glacé with Coulis Sauce

Wines:

Apéritif—Pineau de Charentes

With the Terrine—Tavel Rosé, La Marcelle, Chapoutier, 1979

With the Paupiettes—Meursault, Louis Latour, 1979

With the Glacé—Champagne, Taittinger, La Française, Brut, 1975

Tony Greco, Owner

Pierre Chambrin, Executive Chef

George Torchio, Maître d'

MAISON BLANCHE

Maison Blanche is an integral part of the Washington, D.C. landscape. Situated next to the White House, it can boast that its regular clientele is as famous as the next-door neighbors: it is a place where people go to be seen. But whether one goes to watch or to be watched, Maison Blanche provides both with the same first-class dining experience.

Owner Tony Greco, with thirty-five years of experience in the restaurant business, describes his establishment as "a French restaurant with Italian warmth." Executive Chef Pierre Chambrin is responsible for the exquisite cuisine. An extremely experienced professional, one who studied in France and has worked in such exotic locations as Tahiti, Pierre would not hesitate to fly in fresh frog legs from France for a luncheon specialty. Perfection is the rule, not the goal, for him. The genuine warmth of the restaurant's staff is born of Tony's influence. Although he claims to be "only 10 percent of the total," his dedication to and enthusiasm for the profession clearly inspires his staff—and all to the benefit of the patron.

The decor of Maison Blanche is one of old world charm with its warm wood tones, etched glass, and sparkling crystal. But the presence of wealth and power happily animates the scene. Maison Blanche is an ideal place to enjoy the best of Washington in the best of settings.

1725 F Street, N.W.

TERRINE DE LÉGUMES

14 ounces shelled fresh peas	2⅓ teaspoons salt
¾ pound fresh young string beans	⅓ teaspoon freshly ground pepper
1 pound new, baby carrots	2 egg whites
6 large fresh artichokes	1 cup corn oil
½ lemon	TOMATO DRESSING
Juice of 3 lemons	(see second page
1 tablespoon flour	following)
1½ pounds jambon semi-sel (uncooked, lightly salted ham)	

1. Place the peas, string beans, and carrots into separate pots of boiling salted water. Cook the peas about 4 minutes, the string beans about 5 to 6 minutes, and the carrots about 8 to 10 minutes, or until all are crisp-tender. Drain and immediately place the vegetables in bowls of ice water to arrest further cooking. When cooled, drain completely and refrigerate.

2. Trim the tops and stems from the artichokes and wipe immediately with the lemon half to prevent darkening.

3. Create a "blanc" by adding the juice of 1 lemon and the flour to a large pot of water. Bring to a boil, then put in the artichokes, cover, and cook 20 to 30 minutes. Let artichokes cool in the liquid. Drain. Remove all leaves and chokes. Trim bottoms until smooth and even. Chill thoroughly in the refrigerator.

4. Remove fat and sinew from the ham and finely dice. Refrigerate the diced ham for 30 minutes, and, at the same time, place the workbowl of a food processor in the freezer to chill.

5. Place the cold diced ham, juice of 2 lemons, salt, and pepper into the well-chilled blender or food processor. Blend a few seconds and add the egg whites. Blend well. Add the oil, a little at a time, while continuing to blend to a smooth purée. It is important that the mixture remain cool.

6. Preheat oven to 325°. Oil a glass loaf pan, a 6-cup pottery mold, or a cast-iron pâté mold lined with enamel.

(continued next page)

7. Spread a thin layer of the ham purée over the bottom of the mold. Arrange neat rows of the chilled carrots on top. Spread a second layer of the purée over the carrots. Line the string beans close together over this layer, reserving 12 for garnish. Spread a third layer of purée over the beans. Slice the artichoke bottoms from top to bottom, so each slice is a small semicircle. Fit the slices closely together on top. Spread a fourth layer of purée over the artichoke slices. Cover with the peas and top with the final layer of purée.

8. Cover the terrine with buttered waxed paper. Set in a large baking pan. Fill the pan with boiling water to half the height of the terrine mold. Bake in preheated oven for 30 minutes or until done. Chill at least 8 hours, or overnight if desired. Unmold by running a table knife around the inside of the terrine. Invert over a dish and wrap a tea towel dampened with warm water around the mold to loosen.

9. To serve, ladle the Tomato Dressing generously over chilled plates. Carefully cut the terrine into slices ¾-inch thick and arrange over the dressing. Garnish with the reserved string beans and serve at once.

Preparation of the terrine requires your attention to detail, but the reward is worth your effort.

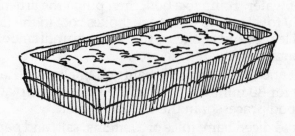

MAISON BLANCHE

TOMATO DRESSING

1¼ pounds fresh tomatoes (about 3 to 4 medium size)	¼ teaspoon freshly ground pepper
1 teaspoon tomato paste	1 tablespoon coarsely chopped fresh tarragon
4 teaspoons red wine vinegar	
¼ cup imported olive oil	2 tablespoons coarsely chopped parsley
½ teaspoon salt	

1. Plunge the tomatoes into boiling water for 10 seconds. Remove with a slotted spoon and plunge immediately into ice water. When cool enough to handle easily, peel, cut in half, and squeeze to remove seeds and juice. Press the tomato pulp through a fine sieve with the back of a wooden spoon. Collect the pulp in a bowl and refrigerate, covered, until ready to use.

2. Just before serving, whisk the tomato paste together with the wine vinegar and tomato pulp. Add the oil, a few drops at a time, whisking constantly until completely incorporated. Add the seasonings and herbs and mix well.

Choose tomatoes with no bruises.

Prepare ahead of time, if desired. Just whisk thoroughly before using.

LOBSTER CONSOMMÉ WITH FRESH TRUFFLES

3 (1-pound) live lobsters
¼ cup imported olive oil
2¼ leeks, chopped
  Scant 1 cup plus 2 packed
    tablespoons chopped onion
  Salt and pepper
1 clove
  Bouquet garni:
    Pinch of thyme
    1 bay leaf
    1 head garlic, unpeeled
    Pinch of tarragon
    4 sprigs fresh parsley
2 fresh tomatoes

3 heaping tablespoons
    chopped carrots
2 tablespoons chopped
    celery
1 bay leaf
  Pinch of thyme
¼ pound top round of beef,
    ground
¼ pound rockfish fillets,
    ground
4 egg whites
2 truffles, sliced in julienne
  Drop of whiskey

1. Turn each lobster on its back and insert a knife behind the head to sever the spinal nerve.

2. Heat the olive oil in a deep, heavy casserole with a tight-fitting lid. Add the lobsters and sauté in the hot oil. Reserving ⅓ cup chopped leek, add the remainder to the lobsters. Add the scant 1 cup chopped onion, salt and pepper, clove, bouquet garni, tomatoes, and 3½ quarts water. Bring to a boil and let the lobsters simmer 8 minutes.

3. Lift the lobsters from the casserole and remove the meat from the shells. Cover and refrigerate the lobster meat for later use. Return lobster shells to casserole, cover and simmer 2 hours.

4. In a stockpot, place the carrots, celery, 2 packed tablespoons chopped onion, remaining ⅓ cup chopped leeks, bay leaf, thyme ground beef, rockfish fillets, and egg whites. Add the lobster stock and bring to a full, rolling boil, stirring constantly with a wooden spoon. Simmer gently over very low heat for 1½ hours. To clarify, remove from heat and carefully skim fat from the surface. Strain the broth into a clean pot through a sieve lined with cheesecloth.

5. Finely dice the chilled lobster meat. Add the diced lobster, julienned truffles, and whiskey to the lobster broth. Taste and correct seasoning, if necessary. Serve hot in warmed soup bowls.

I consider this an extraordinary dish and not simple to prepare. It is not to be attempted by those with little patience in cooking. For people who enjoy the quintessence of fine food, however, it is perfect.

PAUPIETTES DE SAUMON AUX SENTEURS DE PROVENCE
Salmon Rolls with Quenelle Filling and Wine Sauce

1 cup *FISH STOCK* (see next page)	1 egg white
	Pinch of nutmeg
½ cup finely diced celery	¼ cup whipping cream
Salt and pepper	6 (¼-pound) slices fresh salmon
2 tablespoons butter	
½ pound fresh mushrooms, ground	*WINE SAUCE* (see next page)
1 shallot, chopped	6 sprigs parsley
½ pound rockfish fillets	3 lemons, halved

1. Pour the Fish Stock into a small pan. Add the celery and a dash of salt and pepper. Cook until tender; remove from heat and set aside.

2. Melt the butter in a casserole. Add the ground mushrooms and chopped shallot. Cover and cook until soft and tender. Remove from heat and set aside.

3. Prepare a mousse by finely grinding the rockfish fillets in a food processor. Add the egg white, salt and pepper, and nutmeg. Slowly add the cream while processing. The texture should be fine, fluffy, and delicate. Pour the mousse into a mixing bowl. Combine with the celery mixture to form a *farce*. Set aside.

4. Thinly slice the salmon slices. Place six sheets of plastic wrap, 12 to 14 inches long, on a work table. Overlap slices of the salmon on each sheet. Spread the farce over the overlapped salmon on each sheet and top with the mushroom mixture. Roll each paupiette tightly and seal the open ends of the plastic wrap. The paupiettes shoud be long and narrow. Steam the paupiettes for 5 minutes.

5. Remove the plastic wraps and place the steamed paupiettes on serving plates. Nap with the warm Wine Sauce and garnish with the parsley sprigs. Serve at once.

FISH STOCK

2 tablespoons vegetable oil
3 heaping tablespoons diced
   carrots
2 heaping tablespoons
   coarsely diced onion
2 leeks, diced

Bones of 3 Dover sole
Handful of parsley
Pinch of thyme
1 bay leaf

1. Heat the oil in a heavy stockpot. Add the carrots, onions, and leeks, then the fish bones. Let wilt about 5 minutes over medium-high heat.
2. Pour in 1 quart of water and add the parsley, thyme, and bay leaf. Reduce heat, cover, and cook 30 minutes. Remove from heat and skim off foam that has surfaced.

WINE SAUCE

3 small mushrooms
2 heaping tablespoons
   shallots
1 tablespoon fennel
½ cup good-quality
   white wine

2 cups FISH STOCK
1¾ cups whipping cream
¼ cup Ricard liqueur
2 tablespoons butter
Salt and pepper

1. Remove the stems from the mushrooms and slice the caps paper thin; set aside. Place the stems with the shallots, fennel, wine, and Fish Stock in a heavy stockpot. Cook until reduced by half.
2. Add the cream and reduce until two-thirds of the liquid remains. Add the Ricard and the butter a little at a time. Add the sliced mushroom caps and season with the salt and pepper. Keep warm in a bain-marie.

SALADE DE MÂCHE ET ROUGE DE TREVISSE

½ *pound red-tipped leaf lettuce*	2 *tablespoons sherry vinegar*
½ *pound mâche (corn salad)*	¼ *cup hazelnut oil*
½ *teaspoon salt*	2 *tablespoons corn oil*
	Coarse black pepper

1. Wash the two kinds of lettuce well and dry completely. Chill until ready to use.
2. Mix the salt with the vinegar in a small bowl. Whisking constantly, blend the oils into the vinegar.
3. Pile the lettuce into a big bowl and pour the dressing over. Toss well to coat evenly. Season with several grinds of the pepper and serve on chilled salad plates.

Note: The red-tipped leaf lettuce is an acceptable substitute for the red lettuce of Treviso, a leaf lettuce grown in Northern Italy and prized for its flavor. It is occasionally available in the U.S. Mâche, or corn salad, is a great favorite of the French and is grown here by farmers who have imported the seeds. Its small, green leaves are soft and delicate in flavor.

NOUGAT GLACÉ WITH COULIS SAUCE
Cold Nougat with Raspberry Sauce

1⅔ cups sliced blanched almonds

2 cups plus 2 tablespoons sugar

½ cup candied fruits, finely diced

2¾ cups whipping cream

3 egg whites

COULIS SAUCE

1. Preheat oven to 400°.
2. Place the almonds on a baking sheet and toast in preheated oven about 8 minutes, or until golden. Watch carefully, since they can burn easily. Remove from oven and reserve.
3. Place a scant 1 cup of the sugar with 3 tablespoons of cold water and a candy thermometer in a heavy saucepan. Cook to the hard crack stage or 350°. Add the toasted almonds and mix well.
4. Spread the mixture over an oiled cookie sheet. Cool completely. When cold, cut the nougat into small pieces with a large, sharp knife. Add the candied fruits and combine. Set aside.
5. Whip the cream in a large, chilled bowl and refrigerate. Cook 1 cup plus 2 tablespoons of the sugar with 3 tablespoons water in another heavy pot until the syrup reaches the hard ball stage or 250°. Whisk the egg whites until very stiff. Pour the hot syrup into the whites in a thin stream, whisking vigorously until cool.
6. In a large bowl, combine the whipped cream, the cooled meringue, and the candied fruits with the nougat. Line a 5-inch by 9-inch loaf pan with parchment paper. Pour this mixture into the pan and freeze a minimum of 24 hours. Unmold and remove the parchment paper.
7. Pour the Coulis Sauce over chilled dessert plates. Cut the mold into ½-inch slices and arrange on the dessert plates filled with the sauce. Serve at once.

MAISON BLANCHE

COULIS SAUCE

2 pints raspberries   ¼ cup extra-fine sugar
3 tablespoons raspberry
      brandy

Place the raspberries, brandy, and sugar in a blender and purée. Strain the sauce and refrigerate.

Note: The amount of sugar as well as the amount of brandy used can be adjusted to your own taste.

This sauce is excellent for many desserts, especially in the summer.

La Marée

Dinner for Four

La Pochette Esmeralda

Le Soupe de Poissons des Calanques

La Paupiette de Truite Coquelin

La Salade Meli Melo

Gâteau aux Fraises

Wine:

Champagne, Ruinart Blanc de Blanc, Brut, 1973

John Bosch and Didier De Bruyne, Owners

John Bosch, Executive Chef

La Marée's specialty is seafood, and it is special seafood. Its flair unites a touch of nouvelle cuisine with the grace of classic French cuisine, resulting in unsurpassable fish delicacies.

Owners John Bosch and Didier DeBruyne combined their considerable talents and experiences to create this fine restaurant. John's chief role is that of executive chef. Born in southern France, he attributes his interest in cooking to his grandmother's home-cooked meals. This "interest" compelled him to study cooking in France and then work in Paris, in Tahiti, and at Jacques Blanc in Washington, D.C., before striking out on his own. Didier is from a family of restaurant people whose travels enabled him to spend half his youth in Washington, D.C., and half in France. Although his domain is the wine cellar, and John's is the kitchen, they are partners on all other matters, cooperatively working to maintain the excellence of their establishment.

Fresh flowers, soft candlelight, warm brown leathers, and hurricane lamps are some of the decorative accents which contribute to the intimate ambiance. For a quiet lunch or relaxed fish dinner, La Marée is the ideal choice. They have taken the word "fish," and given it a new meaning.

1919 I Street, N.W.

LA POCHETTE ESMERALDA

4 *large fresh cabbage leaves*
4 *(3 to 4-ounce) slices fresh*
  salmon
4 *sea scallops, sliced*
1 *avocado, peeled and sliced*
4 *handfuls fresh spinach*
8 *fresh shrimp, peeled,*
  deveined and sliced
  lengthwise
  Salt and pepper

Pinch of saffron, soaked in
  2 tablespoons warm water
2 to 3 *tablespoons white wine*
2 *cups FUMET DE POISSON*
  (see next page)
1 *tablespoon butter*
  BEURRE BLANC (see
  next page)
4 *teaspoons salmon-roe*
  caviar

1. Preheat oven to 350°.
2. Fill a large bowl with cold water and ice cubes. In a deep saucepan, boil about 5 inches of water. Remove the hard rib from the cabbage leaves and submerge the leaves in the boiling water. Boil 2 to 3 minutes. Immediately remove and submerge in the ice water to arrest cooking. Drain and cool until leaves can be handled easily.
3. Slice the salmon pieces thinly on the diagonal. Arrange the salmon, scallops, avocado, spinach, and shrimp inside the cabbage leaves. Season with the salt and pepper.
4. Close each leaf and place smooth side up in a deep, ovenproof saucepan. Add the soaked saffron with its liquid, the wine, and Fumet de Poisson. Add the butter and simmer over low heat about 10 minutes.
5. Poach in preheated oven 10 to 15 minutes longer. Remove. Arrange pochettes on four plates. Top generously with the Beurre Blanc. Place 1 teaspoon caviar over each. Serve at once.

Note: The avocado slices must fit comfortably inside the cabbage leaf without tearing it.

FUMET DE POISSON

1 pound fish bones and
   trimmings
2 tablespoons butter
1 medium carrot, sliced
1 medium onion, sliced
   Bouquet garni:
      1 sprig thyme
      1 bay leaf
      3 celery stalks
      3 parsley sprigs

2 cups dry white wine
   Salt and freshly ground
   black pepper

1. Clean and chop the fish parts. In a heavy saucepan, melt the butter and add the sliced carrot and onion. Sauté about 5 minutes, then add the fish, the remaining ingredients, and 4 cups cold water. Bring to a full boil and boil 25 minutes.
2. Strain the mixture through a sieve into a clean saucepan and return to stove. Cook until 3 cups of liquid remain. Cool to room temperature before refrigerating. Freeze, if desired.

This recipe can be doubled.

BEURRE BLANC

2 tablespoons shallots,
   chopped
2 cups white wine
½ pound unsalted butter,
   softened at room
   temperature

Pinch of saffron, soaked
   in 2 tablespoons warm
   water
1 to 2 dashes Pernod
   Salt and pepper

1. Place the shallots and wine in a small saucepan and bring to a boil. Cook, uncovered, until about ½ cup liquid remains.
2. Beating vigorously with a whisk, gradually blend the butter into the wine mixture. Add the saffron with its liquid and the Pernod, and season with the salt and pepper. Keep warm in a bain-marie until ready to use.

LA MARÉE

LE SOUPE DE POISSONS DES CALANQUES

2 tablespoons olive oil
2 large onions, quartered
2 leeks, washed and sliced into 4" pieces
2 celery stalks, washed and sliced into 4" pieces
1 large clove garlic, halved
5 bay leaves
1 heaping teaspoon thyme
½ teaspoon fennel seeds
6 pounds whole white fish, cleaned and scaled

Pinch of saffron, soaked in 2 tablespoons warm water
2 tablespoons tomato paste
Salt and pepper
1 tablespoon Pernod
GARLIC BREAD (see next page)
AIOLI SAUCE (see next page)

1. Heat the olive oil in a large soup pot until almost smoking. Add the onions, leeks, celery, garlic, bay leaves, thyme, and fennel. Sauté about 5 minutes. The vegetables should not color, but be soft and clear.

2. Place the fish on top of the vegetables and cook 5 minutes longer, stirring from time to time. Add the saffron with its liquid, the tomato paste, a sprinkle of salt and pepper and enough cold water to cover. Boil for 45 minutes.

3. Strain the mixture into another pot, using a fine sieve or food mill. The mill will extract all the essence from the cooked fish and vegetables. Bring again to a boil. Reduce heat. Taste for seasoning and adjust with more salt and pepper, if desired.

4. Add the Pernod and remove from heat. Keep warm. Serve with Garlic Bread and Aioli Sauce.

Rockfish, grouper, flounder, or snapper are preferred for this soup. Do not use bluefish, pompano, sea trout—any of the dark fishes. Their flavor is too strong for this soup. A provincial favorite, this soup is one that many in France prefer to bouillabaisse. For variation, you can poach an egg in each piping hot plate, and it becomes a meal that, in France, is a Lenten favorite.

GARLIC BREAD

¾ cup excellent-quality
  olive oil
2 large cloves garlic, finely
  minced

8 thick slices French or
  Italian bread

1. Preheat oven to 375°.
2. Pour the olive oil into a baking pan large enough to hold the slices of bread. Place pan in preheated oven to heat the oil. Add the garlic to the oil and cook in oven until golden.
3. Place the bread slices in the hot garlic oil and bake until crisp and golden. If desired, turn once and bake on the other side. Watch carefully to be sure bread does not burn. Remove and serve two slices per person.

AIOLI SAUCE

4 egg yolks
2 to 3 cloves garlic, crushed
  and minced
1 teaspoon salt

¼ teaspoon white pepper
2 cups peanut oil, at
  room temperature

1. Whisk the yolks in a deep bowl. Add the garlic, salt and pepper. Whisk 2 minutes longer. Let sit at room temperature about 30 minutes.
2. Gradually add the oil, one drop at a time, to the egg mixture, while whisking vigorously until the sauce takes shape and holds very soft peaks.

LA PAUPIETTE DE TRUITE COQUELIN

1 *large leek*
½ *pound unsalted butter*
1 *medium-size zucchini,*
   washed and cut in thin
   julienne strips
4 *large tomatoes*
4 *(8 to 10-ounce) rainbow*
   trout, filleted
8 *oysters*
1 *cup white wine*

1 *cup FUMET DE POISSON*
   Salt and white pepper
1 *large carrot*
2 *large mushrooms*
¼ *cup whipping cream*
½ *cup Noilly Prat dry sherry*
2 *lobster claws, cooked, flesh*
   removed, and cut in 8
   thin slices

1. Preheat oven to 350°.
2. Wash the leek, removing grit that has accumulated in the folds. Trim most of the green ends. Dice the white part and finely julienne the green. Reserve the green strips for step 5.
3. In a medium-size skillet, melt 3 tablespoons of the butter. Add the diced white leek and zucchini and "sweat" briefly. Vegetables should not be limp. Remove from heat and reserve. Slice each tomato in half horizontally. Remove the seeds and centers and fill with the leek/zucchini combination. Place the stuffed tomato cups in a rectangular baking pan. Melt 4 or 5 tablespoons of the butter and pour into the pan.
4. Using a wooden mallet or rolling pin, flatten each fillet gently. Place an oyster at one end of each and roll up, securing with toothpicks or skewers, if necessary. Place rolls in baking pan with the tomato cups. Pour the wine and Fumet de Poisson into the bottom of the pan. Season lightly with the salt and pepper and bake in preheated oven for 20 minutes.
5. While baking, peel the carrot and finely julienne. Wipe the mushrooms clean and finely julienne. In the skillet, melt 3 tablespoons of the butter, add the julienned carrot, mushrooms, and green leek and "sweat" briefly. Remove from heat and reserve.

(continued next page)

6. Remove trout and tomatoes from oven and place on a warm platter. Keep warm in a low oven. Using a fine sieve, strain the juices from the baking pan into a saucepan. Over high heat, reduce to about one-half the original volume. Remove from heat.

7. Add the cream, sautéed vegetables, and a sprinkle of the salt and pepper. Return to low heat and simmer 1 or 2 minutes. Add the sherry and taste for seasoning. Remove.

8. Place two trout-topped tomato halves on each plate. Be sure the trout rolls are centered on each half. Place a slice of the lobster on top of each roll. Top all with a generous serving of the cream sauce and serve at once.

The trout must be very fresh; the tomatoes must be of excellent quality. This is an extraordinary dish and it demands extraordinary ingredients. You will find that it is worth your efforts.

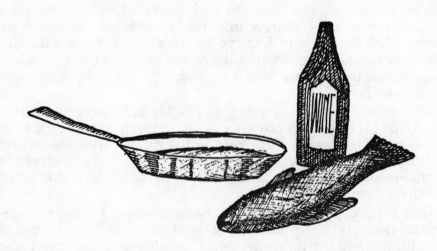

LA MARÉE

LA SALADE MELI MELO

1 bunch watercress
4 large handfuls fresh
  spinach, stemmed
2 diagonal slices smoked
  salmon (about ¼ pound)

½ pound lump crabmeat
VINAIGRETTE DRESSING

1. Wash the watercress and spinach. Dry thoroughly. Pile the spinach on one side, and the watercress on the other, of four salad plates, leaving the rims empty.
2. Cut the salmon slices in about ½-inch squares. Form a "spoke" around the greens by placing the salmon squares along the rims and leaving a space between each square.
3. In the empty spaces, place a tiny mound of the crabmeat. The colors should alternate orange with white around the rim of each plate.
4. Serve with generous dollops of Vinaigrette Dressing.

VINAIGRETTE DRESSING

⅓ cup red wine vinegar
1 teaspoon Dijon mustard
⅛ teaspoon white pepper

½ teaspoon salt
⅔ cup peanut oil

1. In a small, deep bowl, whisk together the vinegar, mustard, pepper, and salt until the salt dissolves.
2. Slowly pour the peanut oil into the mixture, whisking vigorously until the dressing thickens. Serve.

All ingredients for this salad must be very fresh.

GÂTEAU AUX FRAISES

1 *quart fresh strawberries, washed thoroughly and stemmed*
  GÉNOISE
1 *cup Grand Marnier*
1 *quart whipping cream*
¾ *cup sifted confectioners' sugar*

2 to 3 *tablespoons strawberry extract*
2 *cups blanched sliced almonds, toasted and cooled*

1. Slice the strawberries, reserving a dozen small whole ones for decoration. Set aside.
2. Slice the Génoise into three equal layers. Carefully place two layers on waxed paper and one on a serving dish. Sprinkle the layers with the Grand Marnier until moist, allowing the liqueur to seep into the cake for a few minutes.
3. With a chilled whisk and bowl, beat the cream until it holds its own shape. Gradually add the sugar. Beat, adding the strawberry extract when cream is nearly stiff. Spread one-fourth of the whipped cream over the layer on the serving plate. Top the cream with some of the sliced strawberries. Repeat with second layer.
4. Place third layer on top. Spread the remaining whipped cream over the entire top and sides of the cake. Cluster the whole strawberries in the center of the cake for decoration. Or, place a ring of whole strawberries around the top edge and one large strawberry in the center. Press the almonds all around the sides of the cake.
5. Keep chilled in the refrigerator. For maximum flavor, remove about 20 minutes before serving, so cake can warm to room temperature.

This is just one of many "fresh fruit" cakes we make from day to day. They are very light and do not weigh you down after a big meal.

LA MARÉE

GÉNOISE

½ cup unsalted butter
½ cup plus 1 tablespoon sugar
4 large eggs
1 cup less 2 tablespoons sifted
  all-purpose flour

1 teaspoon pure vanilla
  extract

1. Preheat oven to 350°. Set baking rack in the middle of the oven. Butter the sides and bottom of an 8-inch springform pan. Line the bottom with waxed paper. Butter the paper, then dust the entire pan evenly with flour. Shake out excess flour and set pan aside.
2. In a small saucepan, slowly melt the butter. Cool to tepid and allow the solids to settle to the bottom.
3. Combine the sugar and eggs in a deep metal bowl set over hot water. Using a whisk or electric beater, beat about 20 minutes until pale and thick enough to form a ribbon.
4. Using a large spoon, add the flour to the egg mixture in thirds. After each addition, blend carefully with an over-and-under motion, always scooping the batter up from the bottom and lifting high in the bowl at the center. Keep turning the bowl and scooping the batter until all the flour is incorporated.
5. Remove bowl from hot water and place on a dry linen towel. Carefully pour the clarified butter over the batter, retaining the milky sediment in the saucepan. Using the method described in step 4, quickly blend the butter into the batter. Add the vanilla extract.
6. Pour into the prepared pan and bake in preheated oven for 45 minutes. Cake should be brown and should come away from the sides of the pan. Turn out on a wire rack to cool. Do not leave in pan. When cooled, refrigerate until ready to use.

Dinner for Four

Gravlax

Clear Mushroom and Leek Soup

Watercress and Sprout Salad with Tamari Dressing

Sautéed Strips of Sirloin with Hungarian Lesco Sauce

Picadillo

Rehrücken

Wines:

With the Salmon and Soup—Sylvaner, Leon Beyer, 1977

With the Beef—Ghemme, Dellavalle, 1974

With the Dessert—Sauternes, Clos Girautin, 1979 (half bottle)

Nora Pouillon and Steven and Thomas Damato, Owners
Nora Pouillon, Head Chef

NORA

Nora is a restaurant which makes its patrons healthy and happy. The extensive menu of international favorites features additive-free foods whenever possible, and combined with the comfortable and homelike atmosphere, makes for a restaurant of unique charm.

Nora Pouillon, co-owner and head chef, considers atmosphere an essential aspect of a restaurant. She has succeeded in making Nora "a place where people can feel comfortable, where they can come elegantly dressed or in shorts. It is very important that our customers, especially women alone, feel at ease." The furnishings of the restaurant help accomplish this. Large skylights permit natural light to brighten the fig trees, plants, and gingham tablecloths which enliven the scene. Next to the front door, a large window looks into the huge kitchen, positioned so that Nora can watch the comings and goings of her clients, which also makes them feel as if they are entering a friend's home.

Unlike many professional chefs, Nora did not apprentice in the profession as a youth; this may explain some of the freedom and creativity she brings to her kitchen. Instead, she learned to cook through books and trial-and-error after emigrating to the United States with her young French husband. Nora laughingly admits that books weren't enough in all cases: "I had to take a Chinese cooking class. I didn't know what those books were talking about!" Eventually she established herself as a premier chef and opened a cooking school, in addition to writing a newspaper column on cooking. The next and natural step was entering the restaurant business. At the Tabard Inn she successfully developed a luncheon cuisine and met Steven and Thomas Damato, the co-owners of Nora. Their own restaurant followed shortly thereafter, to the delight of all Washingtonians and all visitors to the capital who know they can count on a healthy, home-cooked, and happy meal when they dine at Nora.

2109 R Street, N.W.

GRAVLAX
Cured Salmon

2 pounds fresh salmon	3 cups (about 1 large bunch) coarsely chopped fresh dill
2 tablespoons coarse cracked black pepper	2 tablespoons Cognac or brandy (optional)
3 to 4 tablespoons kosher salt or sea salt	Black bread
1 to 2 tablespoons sugar (optional)	MUSTARD SAUCE

1. Remove the large center bone from the salmon, but leave the skin intact. Place the salmon in a rectangular glass, ceramic, or plastic container. Do not use metal.
2. Combine the pepper, salt, and, if desired, the sugar and rub into the flesh of the salmon. Cover completely with the chopped dill. If desired, pour the Cognac or brandy over the fish.
3. Place a large dish on top of the fish and weight it down with several bricks or cans. Marinate in the refrigerator for at least 24 hours but no longer than three days.
4. Before serving, remove the weights and dish. Scrape the dill, salt, pepper, and sugar from the surface of the salmon until clean. Using a sharp knife, slice on an angle, but not too thinly. Serve four or five slices per person on small plates, with black bread and Mustard Sauce.

Choose bright pink salmon for the best presentation; or, if you prefer, Norwegian salmon, which is light pink but delicious. The marinade is also excellent for curing sea trout and other salt water fish.

MUSTARD SAUCE

2 to 3 tablespoons Dijon mustard	6 tablespoons peanut oil
1 tablespoon sugar	1 to 2 tablespoons chopped fresh dill
2 tablespoons vinegar	

In a small bowl, whisk together the mustard, sugar, and vinegar. While whisking, slowly add the peanut oil. Before serving, add the dill and blend.

CLEAR MUSHROOM AND LEEK SOUP

4 *large leeks*
1 *pound fresh mushrooms*
2 *tablespoons unsalted*
  butter
2 *cloves fresh garlic, crushed*
½ *teaspoon salt*
¼ *teaspoon cracked black*
  pepper
1 *quart Chicken Stock*
  (see index)

½ *cup dry sherry*
1 *bay leaf*
  Pinch of nutmeg
¼ *teaspoon thyme leaves*
2 *tablespoons chopped*
  fresh parsley
2 *tablespoons chopped*
  scallions

1. Wash the leeks thoroughly to remove all sand and trim the green ends. Slice the white parts. Wipe the mushrooms clean with a damp cloth or mushroom brush and slice. Set aside.
2. Melt 1 tablespoon of the butter in a 10-inch sauté pan over medium-high heat. When the butter stops bubbling, add the mushrooms and sauté to brown evenly.
3. Melt the remaining butter in a heavy 2-quart saucepan. When hot, add the sliced leeks, garlic, salt, and pepper. Sauté until the leeks "sweat," or are tender and juicy. Add the chicken stock, sherry, bay leaf, nutmeg, and thyme. Bring to a boil, then simmer 5 minutes. Add the sautéed mushrooms and simmer 10 minutes longer.
4. Serve in heated bowls or deep soup plates. Garnish with the chopped parsley and scallions.

Note: Beef stock, vegetable broth, bouillon, or Bovril are acceptable substitutes for the chicken stock.

You may use onions instead of the leeks, but the taste won't be the same. I often prepare this soup at home. At the last minute before serving, I poach an egg in the hot broth. It makes an excellent vegetarian dish.

WATERCRESS AND SPROUT SALAD WITH TAMARI DRESSING

2 *bunches watercress*
½ *cup alfalfa sprouts, or 1½*
   cups fresh bean sprouts

TAMARI DRESSING

Clean the watercress carefully and dry thoroughly. Remove the stems and place the leafy parts in a deep bowl. Place the sprouts in a fine strainer or colander and refresh under cold, running water. Gently pat dry with several paper towels. Sprinkle on top of the watercress. Pour the Tamari Dressing over, toss well to coat evenly, and serve at once.

TAMARI DRESSING

⅓ *cup sesame oil*
3 *tablespoons tamari sauce*
1 *tablespoon wine vinegar*

Freshly ground black pepper

Combine all ingredients and whisk together vigorously.

The dressing requires no salt, because the tamari sauce is salty enough. Both tamari and sesame oil are available at Oriental grocers and some supermarkets.

I like this salad because it is light and Oriental. For a refreshing lunch, I add sliced radishes and cucumbers.

SAUTÉED STRIPS OF SIRLOIN WITH HUNGARIAN LESCO SAUCE

2 *pounds sirloin steak*
2 *tablespoons clarified butter*

LESCO SAUCE

Slice the steak into thin strips. Set aside. Heat the clarified butter in a heavy skillet. Add the meat and sauté about 2 or 3 minutes or until evenly browned on the outside and pink or rare in the center. Place the strips of sirloin on a warm platter and cover with the Lesco Sauce. Serve at once.

Serve with homemade noodles, dumplings, or boiled potatoes.

LESCO SAUCE

2 *tablespoons peanut oil*
1 *large onion, chopped*
3 *cloves garlic, chopped*
2 *red peppers, thinly sliced*
2 *green peppers, thinly sliced*
1 to 2 *tablespoons Hungarian paprika*

2 *cups BEEF STOCK*
2 *cups dry red wine*
1 *teaspoon marjoram*
Salt and pepper
2 to 3 *tablespoons tomato paste*

1. In a deep sauté pan or saucepan, heat the oil and add the onion, garlic, and pepper strips. Sauté until tender. Stir in 1 tablespoon of the Hungarian paprika, gradually adding up to 1 tablespoon more according to taste. Watch carefully while stirring to be sure the paprika does not burn.
2. Add the Beef Stock, wine, marjoram, and the salt and pepper to taste. Bring to a boil. Stir in the tomato paste until the mixture thickens. Before serving, season with more salt and pepper.

Note: Add more tomato paste, if desired. The sauce should be full bodied.

Lesco Sauce originated as a sauce and dip for grilled sausages. It is commonly used, however, in dishes such as Chicken Budapest and Hungarian Strudel. To prepare Chicken Budapest, bake pieces of chicken in the sauce and serve with generous dollops of sour cream. I often prepare the Hungarian Strudel. To serve four people, brown two pounds of ground pork, drain the fat, and add plenty of the sauce. Butter three leaves of phyllo dough, fill the center of each with the sauce/pork mixture and roll. Bake seam side down for about 25 minutes and serve with a salad. Delicious!

BEEF STOCK

1 to 2 pounds cracked beef bones with marrow	¼ teaspoon thyme
	¼ teaspoon marjoram
4 pounds beef shank, cubed	1 bay leaf
1 cup diced carrots	10 peppercorns
½ cup diced celery with the leaves	5 whole cloves
	1 tablespoon salt
1 cup diced onion	3 egg whites
3 sprigs parsley	3 egg shells

1. Scrape the marrow from the beef bones and place in an 8-quart stockpot. Melt the marrow over low heat. Add the bones and the cubed beef and brown well. Pour in 3 quarts cold water, cover, and bring to a full boil. Reduce heat.

2. Add the carrots, celery with leaves, onion, parsley, thyme, marjoram, bay leaf, peppercorns, cloves, and salt. Cover and simmer gently 4 to 5 hours, stirring occasionally. Remove the scum that rises to the surface.

3. Remove from heat, cool slightly, and refrigerate. When cold, remove the fat that congeals on the surface.

4. To clarify, beat the egg whites and 3 tablespoons water together and add to the stock along with the egg shells. Bring the stock to a boil, stirring constantly. Boil for 2 minutes, remove from heat, and let stand for 20 minutes. Strain into a clean pot through a sieve lined with two layers of cheesecloth.

PICADILLO

⅓ cup dried currants
1½ tablespoons peanut oil
2 pounds ground round
   or chuck
1 cup chopped onions
1 tablespoon chopped
   fresh garlic
1 cup chopped green pepper
½ (10-ounce) jar stuffed
   green olives
1 (3½-ounce) jar capers,
   drained
¼ cup dry white wine
1 teaspoon salt
1 teaspoon ground black
   pepper

¼ teaspoon ground cinnamon
⅓ teaspoon ground cloves
   Dash of allspice
1 to 2 dashes ground cumin
1 tablespoon chili powder
1 bay leaf
   Dash of Tabasco sauce
1 cup peeled, chopped
   tomatoes
1 tablespoon tomato paste
½ (15-ounce) can chickpeas,
   drained
RICE

1. Place the dried currants in a small, deep bowl and cover with warm water. Soak for ½ hour. Drain well.
2. In a deep skillet, heat the oil until almost smoking. Add the meat and brown. Add the onions, garlic, and green pepper. Cook, stirring, until the vegetables are wilted.
3. Add the following fifteen ingredients, a scant ¼ cup of water, and the soaked currants. Mix well and simmer 1 hour, stirring occasionally. Skim the fat that rises to the surface; taste and correct seasoning, if necessary. Serve at once over the cooked rice.

Picadillo is excellent as a filling for enchiladas or served on soft, warm buns like a barbecue.

RICE

2 quarts Chicken Stock (see index)
1 cup long grain rice
Salt and freshly ground black pepper to taste

1 tablespoon minced fresh parsley

1. Pour the chicken stock into a deep saucepan with a tight fitting lid. Bring to a full boil over medium-high heat. Add the rice slowly to make sure the stock continues to boil.
2. Reduce heat, cover tightly, and cook 15 to 20 minutes. Uncover and continue to cook 10 minutes longer, or until all liquid is absorbed. Taste for seasoning and add the salt and pepper, if desired.
3. Fluff the rice with a fork. Sprinkle with the parsley and serve at once, or cover and keep warm in a low oven.

REHRÜCKEN

4 ounces semisweet
   chocolate
¾ cup unsalted butter
   Scant 1 cup sugar
6 eggs, separated

2 cups almonds, finely
   ground
¾ cup bread crumbs
   CHOCOLATE ICING

1. Preheat oven to 325°.
2. Butter a 6-cup rehrücken pan, buche de noël pan, oval mold, or a 5-inch by 9-inch bread loaf pan. Dust generously with flour.
3. Soften the chocolate in a slightly warmed oven or in the top of a double boiler placed over gently simmering water. Combine the softened chocolate with the butter and the sugar in an electric mixer and beat at least 5 minutes until fluffy. Beat the egg yolks one at a time into the chocolate mixture until thoroughly combined.
4. Using a large wooden spoon or spatula, stir in the ground almonds and the bread crumbs. The mixture will be dense.
5. Beat the egg whites until stiff. Fold into the mixture, lifting the batter and turning the bowl until the whites are blended with the chocolate. Pour the batter into the baking mold or pan and bake in preheated oven 1 hour. If a dent is left when the cake is depressed with a fingertip, it is done.
6. Remove from oven and set on a cake rack 15 to 20 minutes to cool. Remove the cake from the pan and cool completely before icing.
7. When cooled, pour the Chocolate Icing over the top and sides of the cake. Refrigerate until the icing hardens.

This recipe, a traditional favorite, belonged to my Viennese grandmother. She beat the chocolate with the butter and sugar by hand at least half an hour, and her oven was slow; she had no thermostat in those days.

If the cake seems soft near the end of the baking time, don't be alarmed. It contains no flour, and the chocolate will harden as it cools.

CHOCOLATE ICING

3 ounces semisweet
chocolate

6 tablespoons unsalted
butter

Melt the chocolate and butter together in a small saucepan. Remove from heat and blend together with a spatula. The consistency should be thin and liquid.

The Prime Rib

Dinner for Six

Bellini Cocktail

Snails in Mushroom Caps

Lobster Bisque

Hearts of Palm Salad

Imperial Crab

Fried Zucchini

Potato Skins

Hot Fudge Sundae

Wine:

With dinner—Chateau Montelena Chardonnay, Napa Valley, 1979

Nicky Beler, Owner

George Gianakos, Head Chef

Garth Weldon, Maître d'

THE PRIME RIB

For a fabulous slice of roast beef, prepared exactly to the patron's specifications and garnished with a pile of freshly grated shreds of horseradish, for Imperial Crab that is creamy and elegant beyond belief, for renowned potato skins served with generous dollops of sour cream, for an extraordinary Bellini Cocktail—for all this and so much more, the Prime Rib is the place to go.

This superb restaurant of American cuisine is sensually furnished. Black walls are trimmed with gold and adorned with black and white etchings. Sconces on smaller walls are colored gold with cream and are nicely highlighted by the bouquet of flowers present at each table. The wall-to-wall carpeting has an Oriental feel, and black leather, high-backed chairs provide optimum privacy to guests. A baby grand piano in the lounge provides the proper background music; polished waiters attired in black tuxedos add the finishing touch of elegance. The Prime Rib is an outstanding choice when one wishes to enjoy one's company, to delight one's tastes, and to do so in a luxurious setting.

2020 K Street, N.W.

THE PRIME RIB

BELLINI COCKTAIL

Per serving:

1 medium-size ripe peach	½ cup plus 2 tablespoons
1 teaspoon extra-fine sugar	champagne

Peel the peach, cut in half, and remove the pit. Place the peach halves with the sugar in a blender and blend at high speed for 2 seconds. Add the champagne and blend at high speed 5 seconds longer. Pour into a chilled champagne glass and serve at once.

We bring in peaches from California, being sure they are ripe and sweet before we use them. We never use frozen or canned peaches for this cocktail.

SNAILS IN MUSHROOM CAPS

1½ cups unsalted butter
6 cloves garlic, minced
½ cup finely chopped shallots
¼ cup minced parsley
½ teaspoon salt
¼ teaspoon white pepper
¼ teaspoon ground
   coriander seed

36 fresh mushrooms
2 cups Chicken Stock
   (see index)
36 canned snails
1 large or 2 small loaves
   sourdough French bread

1. Heat the butter in a deep saucepan and, when sizzling, sauté the garlic, shallots, and parsley over medium heat for about 4 minutes. Remove pan from heat and add the salt, white pepper, and coriander. Cool. Cover the flavored butter and refrigerate until it has solidified.

2. Preheat oven to 500°.

3. Remove the stems from the mushrooms and reserve for another use. Wipe the mushroom caps with a damp cloth to remove any grit. Heat the chicken stock and 2 cups of water in a deep saucepan. Poach the mushroom caps in the boiling stock for 5 minutes. Immediately refresh the caps under cold water to stop the cooking action. Drain well and cool completely. Reserve.

4. Pour the snails into a colander and drain well. Run under cold water for 1 or 2 minutes to refresh completely. Place one snail in each of the poached mushroom caps. Top each snail with 1 tablespoon of the flavored butter.

5. Arrange six stuffed mushroom caps in each of six escargot dishes or ramekins. Bake in preheated oven for 6 minutes. Serve bubbling hot with thick slices of sourdough bread.

It is important to obtain the best-quality escargot, as we do here at the Prime Rib.

LOBSTER BISQUE

1 (2½-pound) live Maine lobster
1 quart clam juice
1 quart FISH STOCK (see next page)
1 bay leaf
½ cup diced celery

2 tablespoons raw rice
1 tablespoon dehydrated vegetable flakes
½ cup light cream
⅛ teaspoon cayenne pepper
Excellent-quality dry sherry

1. Cut the lobster down the back with a large, sharp knife. Remove the sacs from behind the eyes and the dark vein down the back. Cut the lobster halves into smaller pieces. Place the pieces of lobster into a large stockpot and add the clam juice, Fish Stock, bay leaf, and celery. Bring to a boil over medium heat. Reduce heat and simmer about 15 minutes.

2. Remove pot from heat and remove the pieces of lobster. Allow the lobster pieces to cool until they can be handled easily.

3. Return the stockpot to the stove. Add the rice and the vegetable flakes. Simmer 30 minutes over moderate heat.

4. Remove the cooked lobster flesh from the shells and dice into medium-small pieces. Set aside.

5. Strain the lobster broth into a clean pot through a fine sieve, extracting the liquid from the vegetables. Add the diced lobster meat along with the cream and cayenne pepper. Blend well. Serve immediately in warm bowls with a small carafe of the sherry for seasoning the soup as desired.

FISH STOCK

½ pound onions, sliced
1 carrot, sliced
6 sprigs parsley
(approximately)
4 pounds raw white fish
trimmings and bones,
chopped

Juice of 1 lemon
2 cups dry white wine

1. Place the onion, carrot, and parsley in a large stockpot. Place all the fish trimmings and bones on top and season with the lemon juice. Cover the pot and simmer over moderate heat about 10 to 15 minutes to allow the fish to release juice. Be sure to shake the pot from time to time.
2. Add the wine and 2 quarts water and bring to a boil. Skim the broth completely and simmer 20 minutes longer. Strain through a fine sieve into a clean pot or bowl. Cool before refrigerating.

Do not substitute any variety of dark-fleshed or oily fish.

HEARTS OF PALM SALAD

2 heads Bibb lettuce
2 (14-ounce) cans palm
  hearts, chilled

DRESSING
12 thin slices pimiento
6 large sprigs parsley

1. Carefully separate the leaves of the Bibb lettuce and wash well in cold water. Drain or spin dry and set aside. Drain the palm hearts and refresh under cold water.
2. Arrange the lettuce leaves on six chilled salad plates. Center the palm hearts in the beds of lettuce.
3. Pour the Dressing over the salads and garnish with the pimiento slices and parsley sprigs.

Serve as a first course after the soup or, in the European style, after the entrée. The dressing, a great favorite, is also wonderful for a chef's salad.

DRESSING

1 shallot
½ cup garlic vinegar
1 tablespoon lemon juice
1 teaspoon dry mustard

1 whole egg
1 egg yolk
⅔ teaspoon anchovy paste
1½ cups virgin olive oil

Place the shallot, garlic vinegar, lemon juice, dry mustard, egg, egg yolk, and anchovy paste into an electric blender or food processor. Process until thoroughly combined. Continue processing while adding the olive oil in a thin stream until well blended.

IMPERIAL CRAB

1½ cups HOMEMADE
    MAYONNAISE
3 teaspoons minced fresh
    parsley
3 egg yolks, well beaten
2 tablespoons Dijon mustard

¼ teaspoon white pepper
¼ teaspoon cumin
1 teaspoon Worcestershire
    sauce
2 pounds jumbo lump
    crabmeat

1. Preheat oven to 375°. Lightly butter six fluted baking shells.
2. In a large mixing bowl, combine all the ingredients except the crab-meat. Mix well so that all flavors are blended.
3. Carefully remove all cartilage from the crabmeat without breaking apart the lumps. Place the crabmeat in the bowl containing the mayonnaise mixture and gently combine.
4. Pile into the buttered shells. Bake in preheated oven about 10 to 15 minutes, or until hot and bubbly and lightly browned. Watch carefully to prevent burning.

Imperial Crab has brought us almost as much acclaim as our roast beef and potato skins. It is a favorite of both our lunch and dinner patrons.

HOMEMADE MAYONNAISE

4 egg yolks
½ teaspoon salt
⅛ teaspoon white pepper
    Dash of cayenne
2 teaspoons white wine
    vinegar

1 teaspoon Dijon mustard
2 cups vegetable oil, at room
    temperature

1. Place the yolks in a stainless steel bowl and add the salt, pepper, cayenne, vinegar, and mustard. Let sit for 30 minutes.
2. Blend with a whisk for 1 or 2 minutes. Gradually add the oil in a steady stream while whisking constantly. The mayonnaise will become thick and stiff.
3. Whisk in 1 tablespoon of boiling water to seal. Refrigerate.

FRIED ZUCCHINI

6 zucchini	½ teaspoon salt
Corn oil	¼ teaspoon pepper
3 eggs, beaten	All-purpose flour

1. Wash the zucchini and remove the tips on both ends; do not peel. Using a long, thin knife, slice the zucchini lengthwise into julienne strips not more than ⅜ inch thick. Place the zucchini strips in a bowl of salted ice water and soak for 5 minutes. Drain and pat dry with paper towels.
2. Using a deep-fat fryer or a deep saucepan and a thermometer, heat about 4 inches of the corn oil to a temperature of 350° to 375°.
3. Combine the eggs, 2 tablespoons water, salt, and pepper in a mixing bowl. Lay a small pile of the flour on a sheet of waxed paper. Dip a few slices of the zucchini in the egg mixture, then dredge in the flour. Fry the zucchini until golden brown. Drain on paper towels to remove excess grease. Arrange on a hot platter and serve immediately.

Our patrons like this dish second only to the potato skins!

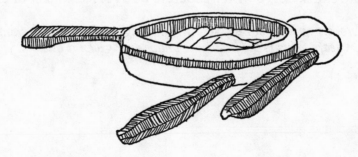

POTATO SKINS

12 large Idaho potatoes	Kosher salt
Corn oil	1 pint sour cream

1. Preheat oven to 425°.
2. Wash the potatoes well and pat dry. Wrap in aluminum foil and bake in preheated oven about 30 minutes until half done. Remove from oven and release the foil so the heat can escape to let the potatoes cool until they can be handled easily.
3. Slice each potato in half lengthwise. Using a soup spoon, scoop out the center, leaving small patches of potato attached to the skin.
4. Pour the corn oil into a deep-fat fryer or deep saucepan with a thermometer to a depth of 4 inches and heat to 350°. Cut the skin halves into two long pieces, so that each whole potato skin yields four pieces. When the oil is hot, drop in a few pieces and deep-fry about 4 to 5 minutes until the edges are golden but the patches of potato are still white. Remove with a large skimmer or slotted spoon and drain on paper towels. Top with more paper towels so most of the grease is absorbed. Sprinkle with the kosher salt. If desired, place in a shallow baking pan and keep warm in a 200° oven for no longer than 1 hour.
5. Line a bread or pastry basket with napkins and fill with the fried potato skins. Serve with a separate bowl of ice-cold sour cream.

My brother and I have been serving our original fried potato skins recipe for fifteen years. This is the first time I have ever given it out!

HOT FUDGE SUNDAE

2 (12-ounce) jars excellent-
  quality fudge sauce
1 (1-pound) loaf pound cake
½ gallon vanilla ice cream
  (preferably Häagen-Dazs)

Amaretto di Saronno
  liqueur
Maraschino cherries
  with stems

1. Chill six sundae glasses.
2. Scoop the fudge sauce into the top of a double boiler and heat over simmering water. Keep warm.
3. Using a long bread knife, trim the crust from the pound cake, then slice six squares large enough to fit into the bottoms of the sundae glasses.
4. Put a cake slice into the bottom of each glass. Top each with a generous scoop of the vanilla ice cream. Ladle the hot fudge sauce over the ice cream and top with a second scoop. Add a healthy dash of the Amaretto de Saronno over each scoop then another serving of the hot fudge sauce. Garnish with the cherries and serve at once.

We do not make our own fudge sauce but use a good-quality commercial sauce that is not available to retail grocers. If you have a favorite recipe, by all means use it.

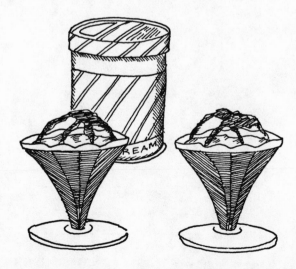

Rive Gauche

Dinner for Four

Coquilles St. Jacques à la Vapeur

Soupe aux Champignons Sauvages

Filet de Veau à la Crème de Ciboulette

Mousse de Carrottes

Salade Julienne d'Endive

Mousse au Chocolat Amer et Miel

Wines:

With the Coquilles—Muscadet

With the Veal—Gevrey-Chambertin, 1976

With the Mousse—Domaine Chandon, Blanc de Noirs

Michel Laudier, Owner and Executive Chef

M ichel Laudier, owner and executive chef of the Rive Gauche, likes to date the beginnings of his lifelong career in cooking to age seven, when he collected strawberries for his grandmother. His formal apprenticeship, however, began in his native Normandy when he was fourteen years old. Three years later, he gained more knowledge and experience by working at various restaurants in France, until his military appointment as chef for the general in charge of French forces in Germany. Following his service, Michel worked at the Plaza Athénée Hotel in Paris where an American guest propitiously offered him a job. Two weeks later, he was in the kitchen of the Rive Gauche; several years later, having helped orchestrate its relocation from the corner of Wisconsin & M Streets to the Georgetown Inn, and having eventually assumed sole ownership, Michel is still there, still making it one of the most exquisite Washington D.C. dining establishments.

The restaurant purposely changed little when it moved, maintaining the same decor, even the same chandeliers. Thus, after an absence of twenty years, a patron will discover at the Rive Gauche the same luxury, attentive personnel, and creative menus as that at the original location. But at the same time, the restaurant continues to grow. A pleasantly dimly lit cocktail lounge has been added, for example, where the fur-clad mingle with the casually attired, where all can relax and await an outstanding meal.

The menu at the Rive Gauche is unlike any other. Michel describes it as "personal cuisine, a mixture of all I learned from all the best everywhere I worked and studied, combined with my own tastes now, and my training in classical French, of course. But, not nouvelle, not classical —just personal cuisine." The recipes included here reveal the enormous creativity of that "personal cuisine."

The latest addition to the Rive Gauche, a Sunday brunch, has already received recognition throughout Washington, D.C., as another realization of the excellence that is the Rive Gauche. This restaurant grows and changes, like the tastes and desires of its clientele, but never suffers in the development. Like Michel, its experience and professionalism assures one of a unique and thoroughly satisfying dining experience.

1312 Wisconsin Avenue, N.W.

COQUILLES ST. JACQUES A LA VAPEUR

1 *pound fresh sea scallops*
⅓ *leek*
½ *stalk celery*
½ *carrot*

Muscadet wine
Salt and pepper
Fresh, chopped chives
BEURRE FONDU

1. Clean the scallops thoroughly. Place in a bowl and refrigerate.
2. Slice the leek, celery, and carrot into julienne strips ⅛ by 2 inches long. Set aside.
3. In the bottom of a couscous pot, vegetable steamer, or saucepan fitted with a steamer basket, pour the Muscadet to a depth of ¼ inch. Arrange the scallops in a single layer in the steamer basket and cover with the julienned vegetables. Season the vegetables and scallops with salt and pepper and sprinkle with the chopped chives. Bring the wine to a boil, cover and steam 3 to 5 minutes, or until the scallops are no longer translucent. Serve immediately with the Beurre Fondu.

This is a light appetizer, one that encourages the appetite without cloying the palate. It is wonderful served for brunch!

BEURRE FONDU

Juice of ½ lemon
⅓ *pound unsalted butter,*
   at room temperature

Salt and pepper

1. Place ½ cup water and the lemon juice in a saucepan and cook until reduced to one-third the original volume. Reduce heat to low and gradually add the butter, whisking constantly so that it is incorporated completely and becomes a light emulsion.
2. Season to taste with salt and pepper. Keep warm in a bain-marie over gently simmering water until time to serve.

SOUPE AUX CHAMPIGNONS SAUVAGES
Mushroom Soup under Crust

1¼ ounces dried or ¼ pound
    fresh morels
½ pound dried or ¾ pound
    fresh chanterelles
1 quart CHICKEN
    CONSOMMÉ
    Oil
2 tablespoons chopped
    shallots
    Salt and pepper
½ pound fresh white
    mushrooms

2 tablespoons chopped fresh
    parsley
4 (1-ounce) slices pâté de
    foie gras
¼ cup Madeira
    Fresh coarse black pepper
1 pound PÂTE FEUILLETÉE
    (see index)
3 egg yolks, beaten

1. If using dried morels and/or dried chanterelles, soak each in cold water for 2 hours. Wash dried or fresh morels and chanterelles thoroughly. Chop coarsely and set aside.

2. Warm the Chicken Consommé slowly in a small saucepan and keep barely lukewarm.

3. In a small sauté pan, heat about 2 teaspoons of the oil. Add 1 table-spoon of the chopped shallots, the chopped chanterelles, and chopped morels. Season with the salt and pepper and sauté about 3 to 4 minutes or until soft. Put equal portions into four individual soup tureens.

4. Wipe the white mushrooms thoroughly with a damp towel and slice the caps into fine julienne strips.

5. Heat 1 teaspoon of the oil in the sauté pan. Sauté the julienned mushrooms with the remaining 1 tablespoon chopped shallots. Season to taste with the salt and pepper and add to the four tureens.

6. Top each tureen with a pinch of the chopped parsley, 1 slice of the pâté de foie gras, 1 tablespoon of the Madeira, and two grinds of the coarse black pepper. Fill the tureens three-fourths full with the lukewarm consommé.

7. Preheat oven to 450°.

8. On a lightly floured pastry board, roll out the Pâte Feuilletée until ⅛ inch thick. Cut into rounds 1 inch larger than the diameter of the tureens. Brush both sides of the dough with the beaten egg yolks. Place the rounds over the tureens, pressing firmly around the edges to seal completely.

9. Place the tureens on a large baking sheet and bake in preheated oven for 12 minutes. Serve at once.

Note: You may substitute any puff pastry dough recipe for the Pâte Feuilletée. Prepared dough is also available at gourmet food stores.

I serve this soup often in my home. When the crust is broken, the aroma of wild mushrooms will rise to greet your guests. Magnificent!

CHICKEN CONSOMMÉ

1 (3-pound) chicken, disjointed	Bouquet garni:
	2 sprigs parsley
1 leek, well washed	1 bay leaf
2 medium-size tomatoes	¼ teaspoon thyme
1 medium-size onion	1 clove
1 small stalk celery	⅛ teaspoon white pepper
1 clove garlic	Salt (optional)

1. Place the chicken pieces in the bottom of an 8-quart stockpot.
2. Trim off half the white and half the green parts of the leek. Quarter the tomatoes and the onion. Add the trimmed leek, tomatoes, onion, celery, garlic, bouquet garni, clove, and white pepper to the stockpot. Pour in 5 quarts cold water and bring to boil over medium heat. Lower heat and simmer 3 hours, occasionally skimming off the grease that surfaces.
3. Place a double layer of cheesecloth in a colander. Pour the stock through the cloth into a clean pot. About 1 quart of clear stock should remain. Taste for seasoning, adding a pinch of salt if desired.

FILET DE VEAU A LA CRÈME DE CIBOULETTE
Veal Slices in a Madeira Cream Sauce

2 tablespoons butter	1 tablespoon chopped shallots
12 (2¼-ounce) slices veal tenderloin	½ cup Madeira wine
½ cup all-purpose flour	2 cups whipping cream
Salt and pepper	⅓ cup chopped fresh chives

1. Heat the butter in a sauté pan without browning. Coat the veal slices lightly with the flour and season to taste with the salt and pepper. Sauté the slices of veal about 5 minutes on each side. Remove to a warm serving platter and keep warm.

2. Remove most of the grease from the pan. Add the chopped shallots and sauté for 5 seconds. Add the Madeira and reduce by about one-third. Add the cream and cook, stirring well, until the mixture begins to thicken. Add the fresh chopped chives, correct the seasoning, and pour over the warm veal slices. Serve immediately.

Some would complain that this dish is not simple. Yet in classic French cuisine, it is very simple and, I believe, considered one of the best! Of course, it is essential that all ingredients be fresh and of excellent quality.

MOUSSE DE CAROTTES
Creamed Purée of Carrots

1 pound carrots, peeled
  and coarsely chopped
  Salt
3 tablespoons clarified
  butter (approximately)

¾ cup whipping cream
  White pepper

1. Place the carrots in a small saucepan, cover with cold water, and add ½ teaspoon of the salt. Bring to a boil, lower the heat, and simmer 30 minutes. Drain well and purée in a food processor or electric blender until very fine.
2. Heat the clarified butter in a sauté pan. Add the puréed carrots, cooking until all excess liquid has evaporated. Add the cream and cook until the mixture has thickened. Season carefully with the salt and white pepper and serve.

Again my love of the foods of Normandy! This is not heavy; the cream just serves as a binder. Be sure you have ample clarified butter to completely cover the bottom of your sauté pan. It is always best to keep some extra clarified butter at hand.

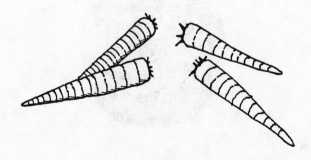

SALADE JULIENNE D'ENDIVE
Endive and Swiss Cheese Salad

1 pound fresh Belgian endive	Salt and pepper to taste
¼ pound Swiss cheese	1 tablespoon wine vinegar
	½ cup hazelnut oil

1. Wash the endive completely and dry well. Cut into fine julienne strips and put in a salad bowl.
2. Slice the Swiss cheese into julienne strips and pile on top of the endive.
3. In a small bowl, combine the salt and pepper and vinegar, stirring constantly for 1 to 2 minutes. Add the oil in a slow stream, whisking constantly until thoroughly blended with the vinegar.
4. Pour the dressing over the salad, toss well to coat evenly, and divide between four chilled plates.

If you are unable to find hazelnut oil, use walnut oil or an oil that has personality. This salad is wonderfully simple and simply wonderful!

MOUSSE AU CHOCOLAT AMER ET MIEL
Chocolate Mousse with Cream and Honey

2 cups whipping cream, well chilled

3 ounces unsweetened chocolate

6 tablespoons honey

1 egg, beaten

1. The day before serving, scald 2 tablespoons of the cream and allow to cool slightly.
2. Gradually melt the chocolate in the top of a double boiler placed over simmering water.
3. In a small saucepan, heat the honey over low heat about 4 minutes, or until syrupy. Remove from heat. Mix the beaten egg with the warmed honey, beating until the honey cools. Mix the egg/honey combination into the melted chocolate. Add the scalded cream, pour into a shallow pan, cover loosely, and refrigerate overnight.
4. About two hours before serving, remove the chocolate mixture from the refrigerator and soften to room temperature. Pour into a heavy mixing bowl and whip until smooth. Pour the remaining well-chilled cream into the whipped chocolate and beat vigorously until the mousse becomes light and high and holds its own shape.
5. Using a pastry bag and piping tube, pipe the mousse into tall parfait glasses or into pretty dessert dishes. Refrigerate until ready to serve.

Served with an excellent champagne, this dessert is the perfect finale to a special meal. Be sure to seek out the best chocolate. It makes a tremendous difference in the finished product.

SAKURA PALACE

Dinner for Six

Nigiri Sushi

Maki Sushi

Chicken and Scallop Kushizashi

Suimono

Shrimp Tempura with Vegetables

Negimaki

Salmon Teriyaki

Fresh Fruit

Beverages:

Before and during dinner—warm Saké

With dinner—Kirin beer

Frank and Kazuko Kuge, Owners
Frank Kuge, Executive Chef
Isao Takahashi, Head Chef

SAKURA PALACE

The Sakura Palace is owned and operated by Frank Kuge, an American of Japanese descent, whose family moved to Japan when he was one year old. He returned when he was fifteen to his native California, where he later endured a tragic circumstance to which he attributes his motivation for opening a restaurant. He was held in an internment camp for one year during World War II. The isolation and sense of misunderstanding he felt there compelled him to establish the Sakura Palace ten years ago, in the hopes of educating those who do not appreciate the beauty and finesse of the Japanese culture. A remarkable man, a remarkable story, and a remarkable restaurant.

When the Sakura Palace opened, it offered some Chinese foods but since that time has grown to specialize exclusively in Japanese cuisine, served in an Japanese manner. Waitresses in kimonos present warm towels dowsed with scent to the guests before serving Sushi. For those uninitiated to the delights of this raw fish specialty, Sukiyaki and Tempura are prepared just as carefully and deliciously. For parties of eight or eighty, three banquet menus include fifteen chef specialties, each course selected to complement all fourteen others.

Whether one dines seated on the floor in a private room, in the Sushi Bar where the food is prepared in the front of the patrons, or in the spacious dining room, one is sure to experience at the Sakura Palace the best of Japanese cuisine and culture.

7926 Georgia Avenue
Silver Spring, Maryland

NIGIRI SUSHI

2 pounds fresh raw fish (select tuna, sea bass, flounder, salmon, or snapper)

1 tablespoon su (approximately)

SUSHI (see next page)

1 tablespoon wasabi paste (approximately)

5 cooked medium-size shrimp, butterflied

PICKLED GINGER SLICES (see next page)

1 cup Japanese soy sauce

1. Slice the raw fish into strips measuring about ½ by 2 inches. Keep moist in plastic wrap.
2. Dampen the fingers and palms of both hands with the su. Gently roll the Sushi into bite-size egg shapes. Do not squeeze or pack the rice together. Spread just a dab of the wasabi, or less than ⅛ teaspoon, on each egg shape. Lay a strip of the raw fish or a butterflied shrimp on each dab of the wasabi. Press the fish or shrimp into the rice so that it adheres.
3. Attractively arrange the sushi eggs covered with the strips of fish and the shrimp on a serving platter. Garnish the platter with a mound of the Pickled Ginger Slices and about ½ teaspoon of the wasabi.
4. Mix about ⅛ teaspoon of the wasabi with the soy sauce. Taste and add more paste, if desired. Pour into small saucers for dipping. Serve at once.

Note: Wasabi, a stinging hot, green horseradish root, is virtually impossible to find in the United States. It is available at Oriental markets, however, in tubes of paste or tins of powder. To reconstitute the powder, put about a teaspoon of powder in a bowl and add a little tepid water. Add more powder or water as needed to form a thick paste. Mix until smooth, cover, and let stand about 10 minutes.

Su is rice vinegar.

Connoisseurs of Nigiri Sushi select exceptionally fresh fish in season. They also prefer to eat the Sushi with their fingers instead of using chopsticks. Each delicate egg shape is picked up and turned over so that the fish is on the bottom. It is thus dipped into the soy sauce. The Sushi tends to fall apart if the rice side is dipped first.

SUSHI

3 cups medium-grain rice	2 teaspoons salt
6 tablespoons rice vinegar	1 teaspoon monosodium
4½ tablespoons sugar	glutamate

1. Rinse the rice repeatedly under cold water, lifting and stirring the grains several times, until the rinse water becomes clear. Drain.
2. Place the rice in a heavy saucepan with a secure lid. Add 3 cups water and let soak for 1 hour.
3. Place the pan over medium-high heat, cover, and bring to a quick boil. Reduce heat to very low and simmer for 15 minutes. Do not remove the lid at any time. Turn off heat and let the rice steam about 10 minutes. Remove from stove and let steam 10 minutes longer. Remove lid and fluff with a fork.
4. While the rice is cooking, combine the vinegar, sugar, salt, and monosodium glutamate in a non-aluminum saucepan. Stirring constantly, heat until the sugar dissolves. Set aside.
5. Transfer the cooked rice to a deep stainless steel bowl. Pour the vinegar sauce over and toss lightly with a fork or a wet rice paddle until all the rice is coated and takes on a lustrous sheen.

Rice is a traditional staple in Japan and throughout the Orient. It is served in varied forms for every occasion. On the New Year, for instance, it is steamed and pounded into a paste-like substance, then shaped into cakes or balls. Sushi, or vinegared rice, is used for making Nigiri and Maki.

PICKLED GINGER SLICES

1 large gingerroot	1½ tablespoons sugar
½ cup rice vinegar	

1. Pour scalding water over the ginger, but do not parboil. Cool and peel. Cut into paper-thin slices against the grain.
2. Place the slices in a bowl and cover with the vinegar and the sugar. Mix well, cover, and marinate overnight.

SAKURA PALACE

MAKI SUSHI

6 (4" x 7") sheets nori
Su
2 cups Sushi
Wasabi
1 cucumber, peeled, seeded,
and thinly sliced

½ pound fresh raw fish, cut
in thin strips
1 avocado, peeled and cut
in thin strips
Japanese soy sauce

1. Lay out a special 10 by 9½-inch bamboo mat called a *sudaré* to roll the sushi.
2. Dry the sheets of nori over low heat.
3. Place one sheet of the nori shiny side down on the mat. Dampen the hands with a little su. Spread a healthy handful of the sushi over the nori to cover the entire surface. Take a dab of the wasabi and drop tiny portions here and there over the sushi; then carefully spread the wasabi to cover the sushi.
4. Lay horizontal rows of the cucumber, raw fish, and avocado one above the other on the sushi, leaving one-fourth of the rice uncovered on the far edge.
5. Roll the sushi and fillings carefully from the bottom to the top. Wrap the mat tightly around the roll so it is shaped in an even cylinder. Press down on the mat firmly, but not too hard, so that the rice sticks to the filling. Unroll gently and carefully remove the mat.
6. Repeat step 3 through step 5, using the remaining sheets of nori.
7. Using a razor-sharp knife, dip the point in a little cold water and allow the moisture to run down the blade. Cut the maki rolls in 1½-inch slices. Cut straight down and away. Do not saw back and forth.
8. Arrange the slices filling side up on a serving platter. Serve at once with small saucers of soy sauce and wasabi.

Nori is seaweed and available in packages at Japanese markets.

The sushi fillings are merely suggestions and may be used individually or in combination. Other fillings such as cooked spinach, crabmeat, and mushrooms may be substituted freely. In Japan, Maki Sushi is traditional. But because meat is so scarce and expensive, we use mostly vegetables and even scrambled eggs.

CHICKEN AND SCALLOP KUSHIZASHI

1½ pounds boned chicken meat,
    cut into 1" cubes
2 bunches green onions,
    cut in 2" pieces
1 pound medium-size
    scallops

TERI SAUCE
6 broccoli florets
2 tomatoes, sliced
1 orange, sliced

1. Prepare a charcoal grill or preheat broiler.
2. Thread the chicken cubes on three 6-inch bamboo skewers, alternating every second cube with a piece of green onion.
3. Thread the scallops on three skewers, alternating every second scallop with a piece of green onion.
4. Soak the skewers in a deep jar containing the Teri Sauce for 15 minutes. Remove and place on the grill or under the broiler. Cook about 6 minutes, brushing generously with the sauce and turning the skewers after every 2 minutes to expose all sides to the heat. Do not overcook.
5. Remove and cool to room temperature. Arrange the skewers on a large serving platter to look like spokes. Place the broccoli florets and the tomato and orange slices between each spoke. Serve at once.

Kushizashi, meaning "on a skewer," makes an excellent appetizer as well as entrée.

SAKURA PALACE

TERI SAUCE

1 quart SUIMONO (see
    next page)
½ cup saké
½ cup soy sauce

1 heaping tablespoon sugar
1 slice gingerroot
1 heaping teaspoon cornstarch

1. Place all ingredients except the cornstarch in a large saucepan. Heat through and cook about 2 minutes, stirring occasionally. Taste and adjust the amounts of ingredients used, if desired.
2. Dissolve the cornstarch in ¼ cup cold water and add to the sauce. Cook until the sauce thickens slightly. Store in a jar in the refrigerator.

Teri means "to shine." It refers to the gloss imparted to foods by the cornstarch. As a marinade and sauce, Teri Sauce is used extensively in Japanese cuisine. The proportions of ingredients always vary, however, according to personal choice.

SUIMONO

½ ounce dried, shaved
    bonito flakes
1 ounce dried kelp
2 tablespoons soy sauce

2 teaspoons salt
1 carrot, sliced paper thin
    (optional)

1. Pour 3 quarts cold water into a 5-quart saucepan and bring to a boil over medium-high heat. Add the bonito flakes and dried kelp, stir well, and lower heat. Cook about 30 minutes. Add the soy sauce and salt, stir again, and simmer 10 minutes longer.
2. Serve in warmed soup bowls and decorate with the carrot slices shaped like flowers.

Bonito flakes are indispensable in the making of basic soup stock. The bonito fish fillet, according to hundreds of years of tradition, is steamed, dried until virtually petrified, and shaved into flakes with a specially crafted blade utensil. The shavings, which resemble rose-colored wood excelsior, come in cellophane packages and are available at Japanese markets.

Ideally, the Suimono should not have a strong fish flavor.

In a traditional dinner, the soup, not intended to be filling, is served in small bowls decorated with the suggested carrot flower, or, if preferred, a slice of chicken, a small chunk of excellent white fish, or a few Japanese mushrooms.

SAKURA PALACE

SHRIMP TEMPURA WITH VEGETABLES

1 pound raw shrimp
1 medium-size sweet potato
1 small eggplant
1 large onion
12 large fresh mushrooms
12 long runner beans or
    string beans
    Vegetable oil
½ cup all-purpose flour
⅓ cup corn flour

1½ teaspoons baking powder
½ teaspoon salt
1 teaspoon monosodium
    glutamate (optional)
1 egg
1 ice cube
    TENTSUYU SAUCE (see
    next page)
    Grated fresh gingerroot

1. Place a metal bowl and ⅔ cup water in the refrigerator to chill.
2. Shell and devein the shrimp, leaving the tails intact. Cut each shrimp down the back so that it lies flat and forms a butterfly. Arrange on a plate, cover with plastic wrap, and refrigerate until time to use.
3. Peel the sweet potato and slice into ¼-inch rounds. Peel the eggplant and cut lengthwise into ¼-inch slices. Slice the onion into rings. Slice the mushrooms or leave whole, as desired. Cut the string beans into 2-inch sections. Arrange the vegetables neatly on a tray and set aside.
4. Heat the oil in a deep-fryer to 350°.
5. In the well-chilled metal bowl, combine the flour, corn flour, baking powder, salt, and monosodium glutamate. Beat the egg slightly in a separate bowl and add the chilled water. Beat a few strokes, then combine loosely with the dry ingredients. Do not overmix; the batter should be lumpy. Add the ice cube and set aside.
6. Set the foods, batter, a rack or paper towels for draining, and a slotted spoon near the hot oil. Coat the vegetables and the shrimp in the batter, a few pieces at a time, slide into the oil, and deep-fry about 3 minutes, or until golden. Remove with the slotted spoon and drain well on the rack or paper towels. Arrange aesthetically on a paper-lined platter, and serve at once with a bowl of the Tentsuyu Sauce and the grated ginger.

Each guest is invited to mix some of the Tentsuyu Sauce with a little grated ginger. The tempura is then dipped into the warm sauce before eating.

SAKURA PALACE

TENTSUYU SAUCE

1½ cups Suimono
2 tablespoons Japanese
   soy sauce
3 tablespoons mirin

Pinch of salt
Pinch of monosodium
   glutamate

Pour all ingredients into a small saucepan and mix well. Heat thoroughly and keep warm.

Note: Four tablespoons dry sherry mixed with 1½ tablespoons sugar may be substituted for the mirin, which is sweetened saké.

SAKURA PALACE

NEGIMAKI

1½ pounds choice beef rib eye
2 bunches fresh green onions
  Teri Sauce
  Broccoli florets

Carrot slices, cut into roses
Fresh fruit, cut in bite-size
  sections

1. Freeze the beef about 1 hour. Using a strong, sharp knife, cut the cold beef lengthwise into very thin slices and place on a work table.
2. Preheat broiler.
3. Wash the green onions and trim the roots. Place 1 to 2 onions in the center of each long slice of meat. Roll the meat around the onion and lay open side down on a broiler rack. Baste generously with the Teri Sauce.
4. Place under preheated broiler and broil 2 or 3 minutes. Baste again and broil 2 minutes longer. The beef should be tender but not over-cooked.
5. Remove from the broiler and baste once more. Cut into small 1½-inch pieces and arrange on a serving platter. Garnish with the broccoli florets, carrot roses, and fruit sections and serve warm or at room-temperature with bowls of hot rice.

The beef sections should be small enough to handle easily with chopsticks and to fit comfortably in the mouth. In Japanese cooking, every comfort is a consideration.

SAKURA PALACE

SALMON TERIYAKI

6 *fresh salmon steaks*
  Oil
  Salt

Teri Sauce
Shredded lettuce

1. Preheat broiler.
2. Wash the salmon steaks well and pat dry. Lightly oil a broiler pan; place the steaks on the pan and sprinkle with a little salt.
3. Using a pastry brush, baste the steaks generously with the Teri Sauce and broil about 2 minutes. Baste again and broil about 4 minutes longer. Baste once more and turn carefully. Repeat for other side.
4. Remove from the broiler and arrange on an attractive platter. Garnish with the shredded lettuce and serve at once.

The salmon may be served hot or at room temperature.

FRESH FRUIT

2 *large honeydew melons*   1 *whole pineapple*
Long-stemmed maraschino   6 *temple oranges*
   cherries or strawberries   3 *cantaloupes*

1. Cut one of the honeydew melons in half and remove the seeds. Using a melon baller or ice cream scoop, scoop out melon balls and set aside.
2. Slice the top one-third off the second honeydew melon and discard. Using a strong, sharp knife, shape the melon into a basket by slicing long wedges from the inside to achieve a deep zig-zag pattern. Fill the basket with the melon balls and garnish with maraschino cherries or strawberries.
3. Slice the base from the pineapple. Run a long, thin knife around the inner edge to remove the fruit, leaving the sides and top intact. Reserve the pineapple shell with its top and set aside. Remove the core from the fruit. Slice the fruit into ½-inch rings, then cut each ring in half. Reassemble the ring halves to assume the shape of the fruit before it was sliced. Place the pineapple shell over the rings and carefully place next to the honeydew melon in the bowl. The pineapple should look untouched.
4. Peel each orange and trim off all the white. Reserve the orange peels. Cut the oranges into thick round slices. Arrange the orange peel in the bowl and pile the slices on top. Garnish with maraschino cherries.
5. Cut the cantaloupes in half and remove the seeds. Cut each half into wedges. Using a sharp knife, open each wedge carefully so that the fruit is cut away from the rind about two-thirds of the way through the wedge. There should be a loose flap of rind on each wedge. Lift one cantaloupe wedge and slip the rind into a space between the rind and fruit of another wedge. Weave together five wedges to create a mound. Carefully arrange several mounds of five wedges each in the serving bowl. Refrigerate until ready to serve.

Shezan

Dinner for Four

Seekh Kebab Mughlai

Yakhni

Murgh Tikha Lahori

Palak Aloo Methi

Sweet Chutney

Pulao Arasta

Halwa

Beverages:

With dinner—Gewürztraminer, 1978

Mr. Shahnawaz, Owner

Mrs. Maisie Krikliwy, General Manager

Mr. Thomas Gomez, Chef

SHEZAN

In ancient times Moghul rulers brought international cuisine to India. In 1949, when the first public dining establishment in the area of Karachi, Pakistan, opened, it showed its debt to those ancient rulers in the tastes and flavors of its Pakistani cuisine. The restaurant's name was Shezan. Since then, Shezan has grown to include restaurants in nine cities worldwide, in such places as Lahore, Pakistan; London; and New York. In Washington, D.C., the recently opened Shezan is furthering the fame of this exotic and elegant restaurant.

The world-famous menu of Shezan is based on Moslem cuisine rather than the largely vegetarian Hindu diet of southern India. Featured are such specialties as Tandoori Grill Sheesh Kebab Sultani, Yakhni, Côtelette Poulet Mareshal, and Papaya Mystique. Much of the restaurant's success can be attributed to General Manager and Hostess Maisie Krikliwy who helped establish the world renown of Shezan in Lahore and who introduced it to America. Her careful scrutiny of all the restaurant's features assures a diner that the elegant surroundings and service of Shezan will make his exotic meal a memorable one.

913 19th Street, N.W.

SHEZAN

SEEKH KEBAB MUGHLAI
Ground Sirloin Kebab

2 pounds minced tips of sirloin
¾ cup finely minced onion
4 large cloves garlic, peeled and crushed
1 teaspoon fresh gingerroot, finely grated
1 green hot chili, finely minced
2 sprigs fresh mint, finely minced

1 tablespoon finely minced coriander leaves
⅓ tablespoon cardamom
⅓ teaspoon cinnamon
⅓ teaspoon ground cloves
1 teaspoon salt
¼ teaspoon black pepper
RAITA

Place the minced sirloin in a large mixing bowl and add all the ingredients except the Raita. Mix well, cover, and refrigerate for 2 hours. Roll the marinated sirloin into long cigar shapes and place on bamboo skewers. Brush with corn oil and broil over hot charcoals until brown on all sides. Serve hot with a large bowl of Raita on the side.

There can be no substitutes for the seasonings in the marinade, which is pungent and spicy hot. The Raita accompanying this dish will help to cool the palate.

RAITA

1 teaspoon raisins
1 teaspoon currants
1 cup natural fresh plain yogurt
1 tablespoon finely julienned cucumber rind
1 teaspoon finely julienned celery
Juice of 1 lemon
1 teaspoon honey

Salt to taste
Pinch of cardamom
Pinch of cinnamon
Pinch of ground cloves
Pinch of Hungarian paprika
Whole white cumin seeds, lightly salted
Pinch of fresh chopped parsley

(continued next page)

1. Place the raisins and the currants in a small bowl and cover with warm water. Soak about 15 minutes to soften and become plump. Drain.

2. Mix in a bowl with the yogurt, cucumber rind, celery, lemon juice, honey, and salt.

3. Combine the cardamom, cinnamon, and cloves, and sprinkle on top of the yogurt. Sprinkle the paprika, cumin seeds, and parsley separately on top. Chill thoroughly before serving.

Note: The 1 tablespoon cucumber rind should include some of the cucumber flesh.

Raita is excellent as a side dish. It also complements chicken and curry dishes.

YAKHNI
Pakistani Style Consommé

3 pounds chicken and beef bones	1 bay leaf
1 large onion, sliced	½ teaspoon coriander seeds
4 large cloves garlic, crushed	2 large black cardamom seeds
3 slices fresh gingerroot, peeled	2 small green cardamom seeds
1 cinnamon stick	½ pound ground beef
4 whole cloves	½ teaspoon finely crushed dried mint (approximately)
¼ teaspoon coarse black pepper	

1. Boil 8 quarts of water. Place all ingredients except the ground beef and mint in a deep stockpot with a secure lid and add the boiling water. Return to a full boil, reduce heat, cover, and simmer slowly 5 to 8 hours. Occasionally, remove any scum that rises to the surface.

2. Remove from heat and cool. Refrigerate overnight.

3. The next day, skim the congealed fat from the surface of the stock. Bring to a boil and add the ground beef. Cook slowly for 10 minutes, removing any scum that rises to the surface. Remove from heat and let stand for 15 minutes.

4. Pour the soup into a clean pot through a fine sieve lined with dampened cheesecloth.

5. Before serving, bring to a boil. Ladle into warm soup bowls. Over each add a pinch of the mint. Serve at once.

It is important that we use all the bones and leftovers from our meals. They can be frozen and then combined in a deep pot with vegetable scraps and peels to make a stock. So many people throw away the most valuable parts of the foods we eat, such as potato and carrot peels. It is important that we use the bones and leftovers from the preparation of our meals, especially when there are small children in the house. Besides, good stock will always be at hand.

MURGH TIKHA LAHORI
Marinated Tandoori Chicken

1½ pounds chicken	Pinch of cardamom
1 tablespoon plain fresh yogurt	Pinch of cinnamon
	Pinch of ground cloves
Juice of 1 lemon	¼ teaspoon red chili powder
2 cloves garlic, crushed	1 teaspoon paprika
½ teaspoon grated fresh gingerroot	2 tablespoons corn oil
	2 tablespoons butter, melted
Salt and pepper to taste	Rice (see index)

1. The day before serving, skin the chicken and cut into four pieces. Slash the pieces all over so that the marinade will permeate well.

2. In a deep bowl, prepare the marinade by combining all the remaining ingredients except the melted butter and the rice. Place the pieces of chicken in the marinade, turning and spooning the sauce over the meat to coat well. Cover and refrigerate 24 hours, turning every few hours so that the sauce covers the meat evenly.

3. When ready to cook, place over hot charcoals and brush with the melted butter. Baste occasionally with the marinade and turn often. The chicken should cook until nicely browned and well done. Serve very hot with buttered rice.

Note: The cardamom, cinnamon, and cloves should total ¼ teaspoon.

PALAK ALOO METHI
Spinach with New Potatoes

¼ cup corn oil
1 large onion, finely sliced
2 large tomatoes, minced
1 teaspoon turmeric powder
½ teaspoon red chili powder
4 large cloves garlic
1 teaspoon finely sliced and
   julienned fresh gingerroot
½ teaspoon peppercorns
1 pound large new potatoes,
   peeled and cut in finger-
   size pieces

2 pounds fresh spinach
   leaves, washed, drained,
   and finely chopped
Salt to taste
2 tablespoons chopped green
   coriander
½ teaspoon methi
4 tablespoons butter
½ teaspoon cumin seeds
⅛ teaspoon chopped hot red
   chili

1. In a heavy saucepan with a secure lid, heat the oil well and add the onion. Cook until golden brown. Add the tomatoes, turmeric powder, chili powder, garlic, ginger, and peppercorns. Fry over medium heat, stirring from time to time. Watch carefully to avoid burning.

2. When the contents of the pan begin to look dry, add the potatoes and fry about 3 minutes, shaking the pan occasionally. Add the spinach and mix well with a large wooden spoon. Reduce heat and cover to allow the spinach to wilt. Cook about 5 minutes, stirring occasionally.

3. Add the salt and coriander and continue to cook until the potatoes test done when pierced with a fork. Rub the methi leaves between the palms to crush; sprinkle over the spinach and potatoes. Replace the cover, remove from heat, and let stand about 7 minutes. Shake the pan frequently without breaking the potatoes. Turn out on a warmed serving dish and keep hot.

4. In a small saucepan, melt the butter. When sizzling hot, add the cumin seeds and chopped chili. Fry about 2 to 3 minutes and remove. Pour over the spinach/potato combination and serve steaming hot.

Methi, or dried fenugreek leaves, can be purchased at Indian stores. Be sure to ask for Kasur brand.

SWEET CHUTNEY

12	large red ripe tomatoes, skinned	2	cups cider vinegar
4	large red carrots, coarsely grated	1½	cups sugar
2	red apples, cored and coarsely chopped	2	teaspoons salt
		1	teaspoon red chili powder
2	tart green apples, cored and coarsely chopped	2	tablespoons raisins
		3	tablespoons sliced almonds
4	stalks celery, coarsely chopped	½	teaspoon ground cinnamon
	Juice of 4 lemons	¼	teaspoon ground cloves
12	cloves garlic, sliced	¼	teaspoon large cardamom pods, ground
3	inches gingerroot, peeled and sliced into julienne strips		

1. Place all ingredients in a heavy saucepan and bring to a boil over medium heat. Reduce heat and cook until the mixture thickens. Stir frequently and watch carefully to avoid burning.

2. Remove from heat and let cool. Bottle and keep refrigerated or store in a cool, dry place.

Note: Our chutney can be stored safely in a cool place for several weeks without sterilization. We do not can it in sterilized jars only because we make it every week. If you wish to preserve the chutney, however, do so; it makes a wonderful gift.

SHEZAN

PULAO ARASTA
Northern Indian Style Rice

2 cups Pakistani Basmati
   long-grain rice
3 tablespoons butter
2 medium onions, finely
   sliced

1 teaspoon black cumin seeds
1 quart Yakhni (see index)
   Sliced almonds (optional)
   Raisins (optional)

1. Rinse the rice thoroughly in cold water three or four times. Drain. Cover with cold water and soak 4 to 6 hours. Rinse again and drain thoroughly.
2. In a deep saucepan, heat 2 tablespoons of the butter and half the sliced onions. Fry until golden brown. Add the cumin seeds and fry 1 minute longer. Add the rice and stir well to coat with the butter.
3. Pour in the Yakhni and cook over medium heat until the liquid has almost evaporated. Stir once and let the rice settle down evenly.
4. Preheat oven to 350°.
5. When the liquid has almost disappeared, fold a clean white linen towel so that it will fit inside the pot and completely cover the rice. Lay the folded towel over the rice, being sure that it seals in the steam.
6. Cover the pot and place in preheated oven. Cook for 15 minutes. Turn off oven but leave the pot inside for another 5 minutes, or until time to serve.
7. Meanwhile, fry the remaining onion slices in the remaining 1 tablespoon butter until golden brown. Reserve.
8. Remove the lid and the towel from the rice. Fluff the rice and scoop into a bowl. Garnish with the fried onions, almonds, and raisins, if desired. Serve at once.

This is delicious! We serve it with almost every meal.

HALWA
Warm Carrot Dessert

½ pound ricotta cheese
2 quarts plus ¼ cup whole
   milk
   Pinch of saffron
½ cup unsalted butter
3 large carrots, pared and
   grated
¼ pound dates, chopped
½ cup sugar

⅛ teaspoon ground green
   cardamom or 12 green
   cardamom seeds,
   pounded coarsely
1 tablespoon sliced almonds
1 sheet silver leaf
   Pistachio nuts, finely
   sliced

1. Blend the ricotta cheese in an electric blender until smooth. Set aside.
2. Heat the ¼ cup milk until scalding. Dissolve the saffron in the hot milk and set aside.
3. Melt the butter in a deep heavy saucepan. When sizzling hot, add the carrots and dates. Fry for 5 minutes, stirring constantly.
4. Add the sugar and mix well. Add the 2 quarts milk and bring to a full boil. Stirring frequently, cook over medium heat until very thick. Do not burn.
5. Add the blended ricotta cheese and cook, stirring constantly, until the mixture is very thick and the butter begins to come through. Add the cardamom and almonds. Stirring constantly, cook 5 minutes longer.
6. Add the dissolved saffron and stir to blend well. Remove from heat, cover, and cool.
7. Serve covered with the sheet of silver leaf and sprinkling of the sliced pistachio nuts.

Note: If desired, store the dessert in the refrigerator and reheat before serving.

The green cardamom seeds, if used, are pounded with a mortar and pestle. Silver leaf can be found in Indian shops everywhere. If you have difficulty obtaining it, you can substitute edible silver powder, which is often available in shops that stock confectionery supplies.

T. Gregory's

Dinner for Six

Snails T. Gregory

Clear Crab Soup

Grilled Gravlax

Zucchini and Carrots Émincé

Arugula Salad

Grilled Venison

Maple Walnut Pie

Wines:

With the Snails and Soup—Chardonnay, Davis Bynum Winery, 1979

With the Salmon—Meursault, Clos du Cromin, 1978

With the Venison—Château Lafon-Rochet, St.-Estèphe, 1976

T. Gregory Smith, Owner

Michael Soper, Head Chef

T. GREGORY'S

Nationally acclaimed as the first American grill on the East coast, T. Gregory's has been applauded for its austere yet outstanding cuisine. The menu offers common foods prepared quite uncommonly, such as Sausage and Peppers Bagna Cauda, Potato Croquettes, Fresh Swordfish Steak, and Prime New York Strip Steak. Head Chef Michael Soper, a graduate of Georgetown University who received his formal training at the Culinary Institute of America, brings much experience and expertise to the restaurant. He sees to it that every meal is prepared to order, paying special attention to the marvelous sauces that highlight each dish.

The decor reminds one of an old English pub. Each of the restaurant's rooms is arranged around a working fireplace, the glow and warmth from which are complemented by fresh flowers and soft leathers. The gracious hospitality provided by the staff at T. Gregory's also makes no small contribution to its ambiance. For a first-class meal of warmth and good cheer, be sure to visit T. Gregory's.

2915 M Street, N.W.

SNAILS T. GREGORY

36 escargots	2 teaspoons black pepper
1 pound fresh mushrooms, washed and dried	1 teaspoon salt
Lemon juice	6 tablespoons Pernod
¾ pound bacon slab, diced	6 tablespoons dry white wine
1 bunch scallions, chopped	¾ cup butter
2 cups chopped tomatoes	6 TOASTED FRENCH BREAD CROUTONS (see next page)
1 teaspoon thyme	
1 tablespoon fennel seed	

1. Rinse the escargots for a few minutes under cold water. Drain on paper towels and cover to keep from drying out.
2. Quarter the mushrooms; sprinkle with lemon juice and set aside.
3. Heat a heavy 10-inch skillet and add the bacon. Fry over medium-high heat until all fat is rendered.
4. Add the mushrooms and scallions. Sauté until soft. Add the tomatoes, escargots, thyme, fennel, pepper, and salt. Reduce heat and cook gently about 5 minutes.
6. Add the Pernod, wine, and butter. Cook until the sauce thickens slightly.
7. Place the Toasted French Bread Croutons on six small plates. Spoon the escargot over the croutons and serve at once.

For many years Americans have known snails only in the shells, filled with garlic and butter. It is pleasant to find that there is more and more acceptance of this food in other forms. This recipe is my favorite! It is simple to follow and a wonderful way to begin a meal.

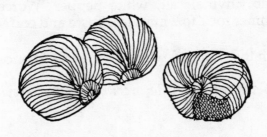

TOASTED FRENCH BREAD CROUTONS

6 thin slices French bread	3 tablespoons unsalted butter, softened at room temperature

1. Preheat oven to 300°.
2. Spread each slice of bread with ½ tablespoon of the butter.
3. Place the slices on a baking sheet or piece of aluminum foil and bake in preheated oven until golden. Watch carefully. Remove from oven and reserve.

CLEAR CRAB SOUP

¼ pound sweet butter	1 pound fresh lump crabmeat
¾ cup chopped onion	1 teaspoon thyme
½ cup chopped carrot	½ teaspoon salt
1 leek, washed well and chopped	⅛ teaspoon white pepper
1½ quarts CHICKEN STOCK (see index)	2 teaspoons Worcestershire sauce
1 cup chopped tomatoes	3 dashes Tabasco sauce
1 (8-ounce) can white corn	2 tablespoons chopped fresh parsley

1. Melt the butter in a 4-quart saucepan over medium heat. Add the onion, carrot, and leek. Cook until soft, but do not brown. Add the chicken stock, tomatoes, and corn with liquid. Bring to a full boil.
2. Add the crab, thyme, salt, white pepper, Worcestershire, and Tabasco. Simmer for 1 to 2 minutes. Taste and correct seasoning, if desired.
3. Sprinkle with the chopped parsley and serve at once.

The soup should have a hearty flavor without being too spicy.

GRILLED GRAVLAX

6 (8-ounce) fresh salmon steaks
1 cup plus 2 tablespoons sugar
½ cup plus 1 tablespoon salt
1 bunch fresh dill, chopped
1 large onion, thinly sliced
2 lemons
DILL SAUCE
(see next page)

1. Two days before planning to serve, wash the steaks and dry well. Place in a glass or stainless steel shallow pan. Do not overlap or layer one steak on top of another.
2. Combine the sugar and salt. Coat the steaks well on each side. Cover with the dill and onion slices.
3. Squeeze the juice from the lemons over the steaks. Cover with plastic wrap. Place a pan or similar weight on top of the covered steaks. Refrigerate for 2 days.
4. When ready to cook, wipe off the marinade. Cook the steaks over hot coals for 2 minutes on each side. Do not overcook. Serve with the Dill Sauce.

There are many recipes for cold Gravlax, but this is my own version, served piping hot from the grill. We are fortunate here in America to have so much excellent salmon available to us. To serve this is equal, in my estimation, to serving the finest filet.

DILL SAUCE

6 egg yolks, at room
 temperature
1 tablespoon wine vinegar,
 at room temperature
2 tablespoons Dijon mustard,
 at room temperature

Pinch of salt
Pinch of white pepper
2 cups olive oil, at room
 temperature
¼ cup minced dill

1. Place the yolks, vinegar, mustard, salt, and pepper in a food processor or electric blender. Let stand about 30 minutes, then blend
well. Blending at low speed, add the oil until the mayonnaise thickens.
2. Mix in the dill, cover, and refrigerate overnight.

ZUCCHINI AND CARROTS ÉMINCÉ

½ cup unsalted butter
1 shallot, chopped
1 clove garlic, chopped
4 zucchini, grated

1 carrot, grated
½ teaspoon salt
⅛ teaspoon white pepper

Heat the butter in a 10-inch sauté pan. When the sizzling dies down, add the shallot and garlic. Simmer 1 to 2 minutes, and add the zucchini and carrot. Cook quickly, flipping the pan to coat the vegetables well. Season with the salt and white pepper and serve at once.

The trick to preparing this simple yet elegant vegetable side dish is in flipping the pan so that the zucchini and carrots heat more than cook. Flipping the pan properly may require practice, but it is not too difficult and is well worth the effort.

ARUGULA SALAD

3 bunches arugula
1 red onion
¼ cup red wine vinegar
½ cup olive oil
1 teaspoon salt
   Ground black pepper to
   taste (optional)

1 tablespoon chopped fresh
   basil
3 tomatoes
1 bunch radishes

1. Wash the arugula well, dry carefully, and refrigerate until time to use.

2. Chop the red onion and place in a deep bowl. Add the vinegar, oil, salt, and pepper to the onion; stir well. Add the chopped fresh basil.

3. Slice the tomatoes to yield twenty-four wedges, and add to the marinade in the bowl. Marinate in the refrigerator for 2 hours.

4. Slice the radishes and place in a bowl with the chilled arugula. Pour the tomato marinade over and toss carefully. Place in six chilled salad bowls or plates and serve at once.

Arugula is a leaf vegetable much prized by the Italians. It is popular in the East and gaining in popularity in the Midwest. Many grow it in their own back yards; so to be presented with a homegrown Arugula Salad is to be greatly favored by your host.

T. GREGORY'S

GRILLED VENISON

1 onion, chopped	2 tablespoons brandy
1 carrot, chopped	½ cup red wine
1 stalk celery, chopped	¼ cup red wine vinegar
1 large clove garlic, chopped	1 cup apple juice
2 bay leaves	2 pounds venison, cut from the leg
1 tablespoon thyme	GRAND VENEUR SAUCE

1. Two days before serving, combine the onion, carrot, celery, garlic, bay leaves, thyme, brandy, red wine, vinegar, and apple juice in a deep bowl. Mix well to blend. Add the venison and marinate for 48 hours, turning every twelve hours to marinate evenly.
2. When ready to cook, remove the venison and reserve the marinade for the Grand Veneur Sauce. Grill the venison over hot coals until medium rare. If desired, test by slicing into the meat with the point of a thin, sharp knife.
3. Slice the venison on the bias and serve with the Grand Veneur Sauce.

Though venison is not always available, I try to feature it on the menu whenever possible. It is our house specialty.

GRAND VENEUR SAUCE

½ cup venison marinade (see recipe above)	½ cup whipping cream Salt and pepper to taste
1½ cups BROWN SAUCE (see next page)	2 tablespoons brandy (optional)
2 tablespoons red currant jelly	

1. Combine the venison marinade with the Brown Sauce in a small saucepan and bring to a full boil.
2. Lower the heat and mix in the red currant jelly, cream, and salt and pepper. If desired, add the brandy and mix well.

T. GREGORY'S

BROWN SAUCE

4 pounds beef or venison bones and trimmings	1 stalk celery
¼ cup butter (approximately)	1 teaspoon thyme
¾ pound onions, minced	4 bay leaves
½ pound carrots, minced	1 cup clarified butter
½ bunch fresh parsley	2⅓ cups all-purpose flour
	4 ounces tomato paste

1. Preheat oven to 450°.
2. Place the bones and trimmings in a heavy, ovenproof skillet. Melt a little of the butter and drizzle over the bones. Place the skillet in preheated oven. Brown well, shaking the pan frequently.
3. Meanwhile, heat about 2 tablespoons of the butter in a large stockpot. Brown the onions first, then the carrots.
4. Remove the bones and trimmings from the skillet, leaving the fat. Add the bones and trimmings, parsley, celery, thyme, and bay leaves to the stockpot. Pour in 1 gallon of water and bring to a full boil. Skim all fat that rises to the surface.
5. Reduce heat and simmer about 3 hours. Skim the fat from the stock again and cook 1 to 2 hours longer.
6. Using a fine sieve, strain the stock into a clean pot.
7. Melt the clarified butter in a small saucepan over low heat. To make a roux, add the flour and beat with a wooden spoon until well blended.
8. Whisk the roux into the stock and bring to a full boil. Reduce heat and add the tomato paste. Cook 1 hour and strain again before using.

MAPLE WALNUT PIE

Pastry for 1 (9-inch)
  pie shell
6 tablespoons unsalted butter
½ cup brown sugar
½ cup honey
1 cup plus 2 tablespoons
  maple syrup
2 tablespoons molasses
3 eggs, beaten
⅛ teaspoon vanilla extract
⅛ teaspoon maple extract
1½ cups walnuts, halved

1. Preheat oven to 350°. Line a 9-inch pie pan with the prepared pie crust, being sure to flute the edges high.
2. Cream the butter and brown sugar. Add the honey, maple syrup, and molasses and beat together thoroughly until very smooth.
3. Add the beaten eggs, vanilla extract, and maple extract and beat lightly. Place the nuts in the pie shell and add the filling.
4. Bake in preheated oven for 35 to 40 minutes, or until the filling is set.
5. Cool, then slice, or refrigerate until ready to use.

Top each serving with a big scoop of lightly sweetened whipped cream for an excellent dessert!

209½

Dinner for Four

Kir Cremant

Baked Hazelnut Shrimp

Fresh Racks of Lamb Diable

Zucchini Parmesan Pancakes

Sautéed Cherry Tomatoes

Hazelnut Mocha Torte

Beverages:

With dinner—Pernand Vergelesses, Marius d'Arche, 1978

After dinner—French breakfast coffee or teas from the Grace Tea Company

Jason and Joel Wolin and Rochelle Rose, Owners

Christopher Hawkins and Steven Schumacher, Chefs

The meal is always sumptuous at the 209½, a store-front restaurant located just two blocks from the nation's Capitol. The fixed-price menu changes monthly, being designed so that all the courses, and every taste flavoring them, combine to a single effect. A light appetizer is served first, followed by a hearty entrée complemented by appropriate vegetables. The guests are then given time to pause, to linger over wine, crackers, and strong cheese such as goat, Stilton, or Canadian cheddar. This prepares the palate for the rich, sensuous dessert which completes the repast.

The driving force behind the 209½ is Jason Wolin who, at the age of fifteen, cleaned the classrooms of a midwestern cooking school to help defray the cost of attending night classes. He later studied at a chef's school in Dijon, France, where he learned the particulars of restaurant management. After apprenticing at several Washington restaurants, he opened his own, the Hot Diggity Dog, which he describes as a "fun and current idea." With that success behind him, and the desire to create an unusual and more sophisticated dining establishment, he then created the 209½.

Jason is quick to state that the restaurant's success is due to a group effort. He happily shares the limelight and management of the 209½ with his co-owners, brother Joel and their mother Rochelle Rose. He further believes he has as much a responsibility to his staff as they do to him: "My job is to train and work with young people who enjoy working with food, with the hope that at some time they, in turn, will create something like this. Hopefully it will be a fun experience in dining."

It certainly is fun for the guests. Extravagant and delightful colors everywhere set an exciting mood—colors of the lavender and raisin walls, of the huge glass vases filled with fresh flowers, and of the beautifully hand-painted china. The restaurant's small size of thirty-eight seats invites sociability between the patrons. Those who dine at the 209½ remember it long after they have left, and resolve to return soon.

209½ Pennsylvania Avenue, S.E.

KIR CREMANT

Per serving:

 1 tablespoon créme de cassis
    Chilled blanc de blancs
      sparkling wine

 1 lemon twist

1. Pour the cassis into the bottom of the glass.
2. Fill the glass with the champagne and garnish with the lemon twist.
3. Serve immediately.

This is a sexy drink—it looks so elegant and tastes divine.

BAKED HAZELNUT SHRIMP

20 *large shrimp*
3 *cups chopped hazelnuts*
12 *small or 8 medium cloves*
   fresh garlic
¾ *cup fresh parsley*
1½ *tablespoons butter*
   Salt and white pepper

2 *tablespoons unsalted*
   butter, melted and cooled
   Armagnac
1 *tablespoon fresh lemon*
   juice
   HORSERADISH
   MAYONNAISE

1. Preheat oven to 425°.
2. Peel, clean, and devein the raw shrimp. Cover and refrigerate.
3. Finely chop the hazelnuts, garlic, and parsley in a food processor. Set aside.
4. Butter four ramekins very lightly. Overlap five shrimp in each ramekin to form a pretty pattern. Season lightly with the salt and pepper.
5. Drizzle the melted butter sparingly over each shrimp. Coat with the garlic-flavored hazelnuts. The coating should be light.
6. Over each ramekin, drizzle 3 or 4 drops of the Armagnac and add a dash of the lemon juice.
7. Bake in preheated oven about 5 or 6 minutes until the shrimp turn bright pink. Be sure to watch the shrimp baking. Remove at once.
8. Serve with tiny cups of Horseradish Mayonnaise.

Note: Be sure to add only 3 or 4 drops Armagnac to the shrimp in each ramekin, so the alcohol is cooked out when the shrimp turn pink.

HORSERADISH MAYONNAISE

4 egg yolks	Dash of cayenne
2 teaspoons white wine vinegar	2 cups vegetable oil, at room temperature
½ teaspoon mustard	1 tablespoon prepared hot horseradish, or to taste
½ teaspoon salt	
Pinch of white pepper	

1. In a deep metal bowl, whisk together the egg yolks, vinegar, mustard, and seasonings. Let sit at room temperature for about 1 hour.
2. Add the oil drop by drop, then in a steady trickle, beating constantly with the whisk until a thick sauce has formed.
3. Add the horseradish and taste. If stronger flavor is desired, add more.

FRESH RACKS OF LAMB DIABLE

½ cup pine nuts, toasted
6 cloves fresh garlic
¾ cup coarsely chopped
fresh parsley
2 cups fresh bread crumbs

2 tablespoons coarse Dijon
mustard (preferably
Moutarde de Meaux)
2 (8-rib) racks of lamb,
"frenched"

1. Finely chop together the nuts, garlic, and parsley in a food processor. Pour into a small mixing bowl and add the bread crumbs and mustard. Blend well and set aside.
2. About 1 hour before roasting, use the tip of a sharp knife to score the fat surface of each rack in a criss-cross pattern, about ¼ inch to ½ inch deep. Place the roasts in a shallow roasting pan lined with foil, fat side up.
3. Mash the mustard/bread crumb coating deeply into the scored fat of the roasts. Set aside to allow roasts to absorb the flavor from the coating.
4. Preheat oven to 500°. Place pan in preheated oven and roast for 25 to 35 minutes or until medium rare. Test with an accurate meat thermometer.
5. Serve at once.

If you leave out the mustard in this basic Diable coating, you have a wonderful Provençal dressing that is great as a topping on lamb chops, heavenly on veal chops, and equally out of this world on a tied standing pork roast.

ZUCCHINI PARMESAN PANCAKES

3 pounds fresh zucchini,
washed and grated

¾ pound potatoes, peeled
and grated

2 tablespoons fresh
lemon juice

1½ cups chopped scallions,
green and white parts

¾ cup grated Parmesan
cheese

½ tablespoon chopped fresh
garlic

1 cup chopped fresh parsley

1½ teaspoons salt

2 teaspoons pepper

2 teaspoons sugar

¾ cup flour

3 eggs

1 pint peanut oil
Coarse salt
Chopped fresh parsley
for garnish (optional)

1. Mix the grated zucchini and potatoes in a large bowl. Toss with the fresh lemon juice to prevent discoloration.

2. In another large bowl, combine the remaining ingredients except for the peanut oil, coarse salt, and parsley for garnish. Place the zucchini/potato mixture in a clean linen towel and squeeze out all excess moisture. Add to the egg mixture and stir well.

3. Heat a heavy skillet. Add peanut oil to ½-inch depth and place over high heat. When foam dies down, oil is hot for deep-frying.

4. Dust hands with flour. Form pancakes the size of silver dollars and place in the hot oil.

5. Brown on both sides. Place in warm oven until ready to serve.

6. Just before serving, sprinkle the pancakes with the coarse salt and parsley.

Note: Drain as much excess water from the zucchini/potato mixture as possible, or the pancakes will splatter when cooked.

If this makes more pancakes than you wish to fry, refrigerate the remaining batter in a covered bowl.

Try adding a couple of eggs beaten with ½ cup heavy cream to the leftover batter. Then pour into buttered custard dishes or molds and bake in a hot water bath until the custard is set. Test with a silver knife inserted into the center of the mixture. Or use the batter as a base for baked eggs in individual ramekins.

SAUTÉED CHERRY TOMATOES

¼ cup good-quality olive oil
24 cherry tomatoes, washed
½ teaspoon finely chopped
    fresh garlic
¼ cup chopped fresh parsley

1 teaspoon Herbes de
    Provence seasoning
Salt and pepper
Parsley sprigs

Pour the olive oil into a heavy skillet 10 inches in diameter. Add the to-matoes, garlic, chopped parsley, and Herbes de Provence. Just before serving, place on burner and turn heat to high. Swirl the pan continu-ously over high heat, adding the salt and pepper to the tomatoes. Cook just until the tomatoes begin to sizzle, about 1½ minutes. When the first tomato pops open, remove from heat. Serve at once, garnished with the sprigs of parsley.

Note: The seasoned tomatoes can remain in the skillet with the olive oil several hours before sautéing.

Herbes de Provence is available at all French markets and most gourmet shops. After purchasing, store in a large, airtight jar.

This is an excellent dish that will go with anything. Try serving with an omelet for brunch.

HAZELNUT MOCHA TORTE

1 tablespoon butter, softened
2 tablespoons all-purpose
    flour
9 egg yolks
1 cup plus 2 tablespoons
    sugar
1½ teaspoons instant coffee
    or espresso powder

Dash of Triple Sec,
    Cointreau or other liqueur
2¼ cups very finely chopped
    hazelnuts
1 (12-ounce) jar raspberry
    preserves
MOCHA CREAM FILLING

1. Preheat oven to 300°. Grease an 11-inch by 17-inch baking pan with the softened butter. Dust the pan lightly with the flour and set aside.
2. In a large mixing bowl, combine the egg yolks, sugar, coffee, and liqueur. Beat on high for 7 minutes until thick. Gently fold in the chopped nuts.
3. Using a large spatula, spread batter evenly in the prepared pan. Bake in preheated oven 10 minutes.
4. Place on a cooling rack to cool. When cool enough to handle easily, cut into two equal triangles, rectangles, or squares. Remove from pan.
5. Spread top of the first layer generously with the raspberry preserves. Cover with the Mocha Cream Filling and top with the remaining layer.
6. Allow to "weep" together by assembling about 1 hour before serving. Refrigerate.

Note: Almonds, pecans, or walnuts may be substituted for the hazelnuts, if desired.

"Weeping," or allowing the filling to dampen the torte, achieves the desired texture. The cake will soften slightly. Be sure to refrigerate, of course.

MOCHA CREAM FILLING

1 ounce bittersweet chocolate	¼ cup sugar
2 tablespoons prepared coffee	1 pint whipping cream
1½ teaspoons instant coffee	

1. Place the chocolate, coffee, and sugar in the top of a double boiler. Melt over gently simmering water. Cool.
2. Whip the cream in a deep bowl. Fold the cooled chocolate into the whipped cream gently.

Appetizers

Beverages

Breads, Pastries and Batters

Desserts and Dessert Accents

RECIPE INDEX

RECIPE INDEX

Stocks

Vegetables

THE GREAT CHEFS SERIES

A Collection of Gourmet Recipes from the Finest Chefs in the Country

Each book contains gourmet recipes for complete meals from the chefs of 21 great restaurants.

___ Dining In–Baltimore	$7.95	___ Dining In–Philadelphia	$8.95
___ Dining In–Boston	7.95	___ Dining In–Phoenix	8.95
___ Dining In–Chicago, Vol. II	8.95	___ Dining In–Pittsburgh	7.95
___ Dining In–Cleveland	8.95	___ Dining In–Portland	7.95
___ Dining In–Dallas, Revised	8.95	___ Dining In–St. Louis	7.95
___ Dining In–Denver	7.95	___ Dining In–San Francisco	7.95
___ Dining In–Hawaii	7.95	___ Dining In–Seattle, Vol. II	7.95
___ Dining In–Houston, Vol. I	7.95	___ Dining In–Seattle, Vol. III	8.95
___ Dining In–Houston, Vol. II	7.95	___ Dining In–Sun Valley	7.95
___ Dining In–Kansas City	7.95	___ Dining In–Toronto	7.95
___ Dining In–Los Angeles	7.95	___ Dining In–Vancouver, B.C.	8.95
___ Dining In–Manhattan	8.95	___ Dining In–Washington, D.C.	8.95
___ Dining In–Milwaukee	7.95	___ Feasting In Atlanta	7.95
___ Dining In–Minneapolis/St. Paul, Vol. II	8.95	___ Feasting In New Orleans	7.95
___ Dining In–Monterey Peninsula	7.95		

☐ CHECK HERE IF YOU WOULD LIKE TO HAVE A
DIFFERENT DINING IN–COOKBOOK SENT TO YOU
ONCE A MONTH

Payable by MasterCard, Visa, or C.O.D. Returnable if not satisfied.
List price plus $1.00 postage and handling for each book.

BILL TO: **SHIP TO:**

Name _____   Name _____

Address _____   Address _____

City _____ State ___ Zip _____   City _____ State ___ Zip _____

☐ Payment enclosed   ☐ Send C.O.D.   ☐ Charge

Visa # _____ Exp. Date _____

MasterCard # _____ Exp. Date _____

Signature _____

PEANUT BUTTER PUBLISHING
2445 76th Avenue S.E. • Mercer Island, WA 98040
(206) 236-1982